Essential Elements:
Prepare, Design, and Teach
Your Online Course

by Bonnie Elbaum, Cynthia McIntyre,
and Alese Smith

Atwood Publishing
Madison, WI

Essential Elements: Prepare, Design, and Teach Your Online Course
By Bonnie Elbaum, Cynthia McIntyre, and Alese Smith

ISBN: 1-891859-40-4

© 2002 Atwood Publishing
2710 Atwood Ave.
Madison, WI 53704

888.242.7101
www.atwoodpublishing.com

Cover design by TLC Graphics, www.tlcgraphics.com

Library of Congress Cataloging-in-Publication Data

Elbaum, Bonnie, 1974-
    Essential elements: prepare, design, and teach your online
course/by Bonnie Elbaum, Cynthia McIntyre, and Alese Smith.
        p.cm.
Includes bibliographical references.
ISBN 1-891859-40-4
    1. Internet in education. 2. Computer-assisted instruction. 3.
Instructional systems—Design. I. McIntyre, Cynthia, 1967- II. Smith,
Alese, 1951- III. Title.
    LB1044.87 .E4 2002
    371.33'467'8—dc21

                                                    2002018471

Table of Contents

Acknowledgments

The primary authors of this book are staff members of The Concord Consortium. Our efforts would have been incomplete, however, without the advice, insights, and innumerable tips from additional members of the Concord Consortium e-Learning Group. In particular, we thank George Collison, Alvaro Galvis, Sarah Haavind, Raymond Rose, and Robert Tinker. We have learned the most from the hundreds of participants in our online courses. We thank them all for their enthusiasm, energy, patience, creativity, and willingness to collaborate and share their experiences. The Concord Consortium would also like to acknowledge gratefully the Robert Noyce Foundation, whose generous support made this book possible.

Introduction

Essential (ə sen'shəl): adj. Of the utmost importance: basic, indispensable, necessary.

Element (el'ə mənt): n. A constituent part: as a plural: the simplest principles of a subject of study: rudiments.

Are you, or your university, or corporation starting to think about putting your course on the web? Others do it — why not you? What's there to know, you wonder. What's so different about teaching online versus teaching face-to-face? Perhaps you have been a successful brick and mortar classroom teacher for years, or you have presented at countless professional workshops, so you know you can do this. Indeed, you can, but there is something different about teaching online. This book, with its *Essential Elements* gleaned from our experience in helping to develop hundreds of online courses, reveals just what that difference is. We show you how to create and teach a successful online course. There are just seventeen "basic, indispensable, necessary" parts that make up a successful high-quality online course. Include them all in yours and you are nearly guaranteed success. Is that all there is to it? Yes, it is that simple. Of course, understanding and implementing the seventeen *Essential Elements* may take some work — but that is what this book is all about.

We describe these *Essential Elements* and show you how to implement them to create a truly high-quality learning environment for your students. With tips addressing everything from technology to student assessments, from online community building to collaborative teaming, and from scheduling and pacing to facilitating online discussions, we have the virtual classroom covered. In addition, we illustrate the tips with practical examples from our experiences.

The *Essential Elements* are presented in three sections — prepare, design, and teach — that will take you from the starting gate to the finishing line in this virtual endeavor.

In *Section 1: Prepare Your Online Course*, we cover the necessary preparatory steps — from getting yourself ready to getting your course ready. You'll learn how to create a course outline and you'll consider issues surrounding technology support and quality assurance.

In *Section 2: Design Your Online Course*, we move to course creation — from designing activities that work in the virtual environment to locating appropriate course materials (both online and offline). We demonstrate how to fill your online course with learner-centered activities that engage your students in inquiry learning.

And in *Section 3: Teach Your Online Course*, we suggest ways to make the most of your online teaching experience. We show you how to create course information materials, plus how to engage participants and how to moderate discussions for the most effective participant learning. We also share strategies for effective online assessments.

Finally, we include an Essential Checklist in Appendix C, which you can use to take notes as you plan the design of your course and how you will teach it. We encourage you to use the checklist to mark your progress in different key areas and make notes to yourself on what you need to complete before your virtual classroom door opens and you have virtual students knocking on your web space.

The Concord Consortium e-Learning Model for Online Courses

First, what exactly is an online course? You know it's a course delivered over the Internet, but that definition — rudimentary, although accurate — is insufficient. Let's fill out the definition a bit more. In an online course, students and the instructor access a website. Typically, they log in with a username and password. (Most courseware allows for password-protection to ensure that your course content is secure, and that discussions are not open to any web surfer.) Students access course documents that the instructor has written and placed on the web; they complete online and offline assignments (from reading course documents to reading required books, from searching additional websites to participating in dialogues, debates, or role-plays). To communicate and collaborate, students and the instructor use a "threaded" discussion board — one in which messages are posted to a public space and threaded according to their content. (The word "threaded" means that replies to a main message are indented below that message; replies to replies are indented further, and so on).

While the *Essential Elements* do not describe particular courseware (such as Blackboard™, Lotus LearningSpace™, or WebCT™, to name just a few), most have similar features that will help you to put your course online:

- a special section for posting announcements — students will see it immediately after they log in to your course website;

- a place to put (upload) course information materials (syllabus, reading list, faculty information, etc.);

- another area to upload student assignments;

- a space for students to enter information about themselves, often including a picture;

- assessment features, like automated quizzes and surveys; and

- most importantly, a threaded discussion area for communication and collaboration.

The type of online course we hope to help you create is one in which you and your students will communicate and collaborate on a regular basis. Within the course, students will assess their own growth and learning through group discussion and reflection, peer review, instructor feedback, and self-evaluation. The richness of these interactions will translate into positive and meaningful learning experiences for your students that can carry over into their daily lives.

To fully explain our method for creating successful online courses, we have developed The Concord Consortium e-Learning Model. The Model has nine characteristics that provide an overview of our approach to delivering web-based courses. (They are described below.) This Model will become clearer and clearer as you explore the seventeen *Essential Elements* that make up the bulk of the book. The *Essential Elements* describe the necessary steps to put The Concord Consortium e-Learning Model into practice with these results:

- You will use courseware to display your course assignments and reference materials as text, with graphics, colors, and multimedia to enhance the presentation.

- Your course will have clearly written assignments that engage your students in active learning with each other.

- You, as the instructor, will play an integral role as a facilitator of that learning.

- You will use the Internet both as a resource and as a means for connecting yourself and your students based on your mutual interest in the content — regardless of your individual schedules, geographic location, or physical ability to come to class.

- You and your students will communicate and collaborate on a regular basis in a discussion area that allows for student-to-student and student-to-instructor interaction.

- Students will assess their own growth and learning through group discussion and reflection, peer review, instructor feedback, and self-evaluation.

The Nine Characteristics of The Concord Consortium e-Learning Model

1. Asynchronous collaboration.

Participants don't have to be logged on to the course simultaneously. This means that participants can explore the curriculum at their own pace, taking time to reflect carefully and record their thinking. They work in an asynchronous environment in which text-based, threaded discussion and collaborative problem solving form the core learning strategy. Compared to synchronous tools that are used where participants are all logged on at the same time (chats, shared whiteboards, shared applications, and audio conferencing), these asynchronous discussion groups are less expensive, more thoughtful, and far easier to schedule, particularly across time zones.

2. Explicit schedules.

Even though participants can log on at different times, instructors whose online courses rely on collaborative discussions should schedule lessons within a specific time frame. That way, participants can share similar experiences and insights. One major topic provides the focus for the week, with a sequence of activities, discussion, and reflection. For instance, if the content of a video is essential for an upcoming discussion, then the schedule must specify that everyone view the video clip sometime within a few days prior to the discussion. Each participant is then required to make an initial contribution to the discussion. Over the next few days, participants respond to the comments already posted. The best schedule preserves the flexibility of online courses, while also ensuring that all participants bring similar experience and currency to the discussion.

3. Expert facilitation.

Online courses are led by a qualified instructor specifically trained in online facilitation. Leading an online discussion is a skill that is learned. It is not sufficient to simply assign an online course to even a highly respected classroom teacher. Teaching strategies that work well in a brick and mortar classroom can have unintended effects online, halting rather than deepening dialogue and learning. Like a good teacher in a traditional classroom, the expert facilitator doesn't ask all the questions or provide too many answers. However, effective online facilitators use many other strategies to stimulate student exchange and guide the conversation toward important content, intervening in discussions only when it serves to move the group more clearly toward learning objectives.

4. Inquiry pedagogy.

Instructors create effective online courses with many specific elements that contribute to sound pedagogy for inquiry learning. Graphics, simulations, and role-plays, if used effectively, help learners explore and make sense of content. Course objectives are explicit and matched to the measures used in qualitative assessments. Instructors establish a clear set of guidelines for postings to ensure that evidence of learning is embedded in the discussions.

5. High-quality materials.

Course instructors include the widest feasible range of media and activities to appeal to different styles of learning. In addition to Internet resources, they effectively use books, kits, labs, and other media to supplement online materials. In a science course, for example, students view a visual simulation (e.g., a virtual dissection) or use modeling software to understand a concept. Offline, they conduct experiments with simple materials. Web-based graphics or content shed light on other aspects of the subject. Students engage in explorations, surveys, creative works, and self-reflection, as appropriate. Multiple, short assignments using a variety of approaches and media help preserve course flexibility, reinforce key concepts, and nurture different strengths.

6. Community building.

Learning through collaboration requires participants to take intellectual risks. It is the responsibility of course instructors to proactively design and nurture a community culture in which participants are supportive and honest. The instructor as facilitator establishes and shapes intellectual and emotional norms, modeling appropriate behavior and steering harmful input toward higher learning ground for all. There are many ways to foster this sense of intellectual trust and safety. Providing class time for participants to become acquainted is an essential first step. This is achieved by leading fun ice-breaking activities in the beginning of the course and sustaining a social life for the group with a café or student lounge discussion thread where non-course topics are welcome throughout the course. Written expectations about good group processes are also helpful. For example, instructors encourage participants to use inclusive and collective language that focuses on content when posting to the discussion. Anonymous polls, role playing, use of smaller discussion groups with rotating roles, or weekly online meetings are all effective techniques for building and maintaining group cohesion.

7. Limited enrollment.

There are between 12 and 25 participants in a class to keep collaborative learning manageable. Online discussions need a critical mass, so smaller is not necessarily better. Subgroups with as few as two or three are useful for the intense exchange required to produce something complex, like a cumulative project. Slightly larger teams of four to five work well for focused dialogue on readings, video clips, or other shared experiences. In an online environment, these subgroups remain part of the public record so everyone can glean the insights shared in small group exchanges.

8. Purposeful virtual spaces.

In a face-to-face classroom, the structure of conversation is fluid and invisible. We know or learn to do our social chatting before and after class and during breaks. When the instructor asks if people have questions about the assignment, that's when we ask. Online, course instructors create explicit structures so the community gets what it needs without interrupting the flow of content-based discussions. Typically included are a "Student Lounge," a "Questions about Assignments," a "Technical Questions," and a "Class Meeting" discussion space for debriefing course experiences.

9. Ongoing assessment.

The idea of using one high-stakes test to measure achievement may work well in a closely monitored classroom. Online, however, assessment is a continuous, ongoing process. Instructors find evidence of achievement in participants' daily contributions to online discussions, and learn each student's unique "voice" and approach to solving problems through their postings. The online version of a literature course, for instance, includes regular small group discussions on assigned readings and essays or longer projects, which undergo a sequence of peer review, revision, and final submission for grading. By communicating clear objectives for project outcomes and specific criteria for postings, instructors can hold daily submissions to standards that foster constructive dialogue and learning.

Step Back

Before you get started putting your course online, you will want to take a step back to examine the big picture of what it is you want to do. Start a notebook (paper or electronic) in which you can jot down goals, questions, and comments to follow up on. Talk to other online educators and students. Brainstorm ideas and jot them down.

Most importantly, answer the following questions in our three pre-questionnaires — feel free to answer them in your head or record your answers in that trusty notebook you just started. You did start a notebook, didn't you?

Pre-Questionnaire 1: Goals

Why are you putting your course online? That is perhaps the most fundamental question you need to answer. In this pre-questionnaire, you will examine your reasons for creating a web-based course offering. Take some time to answer each question with care, as your answers will play a large part in shaping the design of your course.

- Why do you want to create and teach an online course?
- What are your goals for yourself and your future students?
- Will these goals best be met by putting your course online?

- If you have taken or created an online course in the past, are there things you would do differently this time around? What are they?

- What benefits and advantages do you think your course will have in the online setting?

- What will you need to do in order to maximize those advantages?

- Do you foresee any major disadvantages to delivering your course online?

Pre-Questionnaire 2: Instructor Training and Requirements

Here you will examine your personal role in creating an online course. Consider the following questions, and — as corny as it may sound — pay attention to the way you're feeling as you answer each question. Are you excited and energized or anxious and enervated? In creating a sensational and successful online course, attitude can be as important as ability! If you are feeling anxious now, we hope to ease that tension and give you confidence as we take you through the steps of preparing, designing, and teaching your online course.

- What makes you — a first-rate classroom teacher or corporate trainer — a good candidate to teach online?

- What skills and abilities will help you create and teach an online course?

- Do you believe that online courses can be just as good, just as beneficial, and just as valuable as face-to-face courses? If so, why? If not, why not?

- What do others who may be involved in this project feel?

- Are you excited about this project? If not, what are your concerns?

- Can you envision what it would feel like to teach in the online environment?

- Do you have any qualities that you think would be an obstacle to your being a good online teacher (for example, easy frustration when technical problems arise)?

- Do you have the time, resources, and commitment to undertake any professional development training you may need?

Pre-Questionnaire 3: Technical Requirements and Administrative Support

In this pre-questionnaire, you will examine the technical infrastructure required to get you online and functioning. Technology and the administrative support around that technology form the backbone of your program — an online course cannot exist in a virtual vacuum. You will need to ensure you have adequate technical support to help with the inevitable challenges and frustrations that technology brings.

- Will adequate administrative and technical support be available to you and your students during training and during the design and delivery of your course?

- Will there be onsite help for students?

- Will you be able to provide administrative and logistical support for your course? (For example, you will need a registration procedure and a way to assign, or change, student passwords.)

- Will you need additional staff, such as a registrar, a dean of students, a librarian, faculty or student mentors?

- If you have taken or designed an online course before, has the technology and equipment changed since then in ways that you should consider before putting your course online?

- Do you know the technology and software you'll use inside and out?

- Do you have adequate server space to house your course and any supporting databases it requires, a process for creating frequent back-ups of the course, and knowledgeable support staff who will help make the technical end of things run smoothly?

- Do you have a plan or policies in place for addressing security, safety, and privacy issues that arise when working in cyberspace?

Okay, you've taken our pre-questionnaires and thought about your "big picture" goals, and you've decided online teaching is for you. You are set and ready to go and you have the technical and administrative infrastructure in place to run your course. That's exciting! Now is the time to get started with our *Essential Elements* — and tips to implement those elements — to help you create and teach your own online course and make it a high-quality virtual reality.

Section 1:
Prepare for Your Online Course

We begin your journey by taking you through the steps of designing a timetable for completion; developing a course outline; and including the basic objectives, activities, and timelines. You will consider course standards and support issues, and begin taking notes in our Essential Checklist (see Appendix C), which you will use to record the many details you will need to complete along the way. We also begin familiarizing you with the concept of the different pace and timing that online courses require, which you will need to keep continually in mind as you structure your course. As you consider the required *Essential Elements* of an online course and begin to put it together, you will build in the key ingredients and not leave success to chance.

Essential Element 1: Prepare to teach online.

The most important part of teaching is you, the teacher. And the better prepared you are, the better experience you (and your future students) will have.

Take an online course.

Before designing and teaching an online course of your own, we highly recommend that you first take and successfully complete at least one online course yourself. Good choices include a course on online pedagogy or one devoted to the courseware you will be using, but any online course counts. This will give you greater empathy for your students' experience when the time comes, help you understand many of the challenges and rewards of online learning, and help you decide whether working in the online environment is right for you. Plus, you'll experience at least one virtual course firsthand, and be able to give thought to how you'd design your own course — similarly or differently.

Be excited!

As with any teaching experience, you have the best chance of being successful as an online teacher if you are enthusiastic about the prospect of what you will be doing.

Panic if you must.

Okay, so you *are* going into this online stuff kicking and screaming. It is scary and, perhaps, feels undoable, because it is so new to you, and may feel unproven. Those feelings are understandable, so go ahead and allow yourself one good panic attack. At the end of it, remember to breathe deeply, and return here. We have been there ourselves, so we understand those feelings, but we have come out on the other side with successes to show for our efforts, and so can you. We will help you make sense of it all, so that developing an online course is not so unknown, not so frightening. Our goal is to make you feel confident and prepared.

Believe in the outcome.

Before you put an entire course online, you should be sure you truly believe in the merits of what you are doing and feel invested in a positive outcome. In other words, believing the desired positive outcome can happen – that an online course can be of equal quality and as beneficial and valuable to students as a face-to-face course – can help ensure its success. We believe an online course that follows our model can be all of these things, and this book is designed to give you the proven tools to make it a reality. We also hope that by sharing our successes, we will give you the confidence to design and deliver your own successful online course.

Do your homework.

All online instructors should be knowledgeable and well trained in sound online course pedagogy. Take a course on online pedagogy, read books and articles, visit e-learning websites and discussion forums, get educated about online education. You have begun that process by picking up this book, but don't stop your research now. Check out our List of Resources (Appendix B) for additional suggestions.

Know your stuff.

As with any course, you should be broadly familiar with the content you will be teaching online. The same is true for instructional style.

You should be comfortable with constructivism, inquiry-based learning, and alternative assessment strategies — all approaches that work well with the online learning environment.

Set aside the time.

If you are new to online teaching, you will need plenty of time to develop your online course. Whether you are converting an existing face-to-face course to an electronic one or creating one from scratch, allow time to learn techniques for coping with the new challenges of the online classroom. You will need adequate time to prepare and teach your online course, so be sure to set aside enough time or encourage your administrators to provide this time for you, in order to guarantee a quality learning experience for you and your students.

Learn to express yourself in text.

In the online environment, without opportunities to smile, wink, raise an eyebrow or use any other body language to help convey your meaning, you need to express yourself clearly and plainly in writing. This means being able to communicate your feelings (approval, sympathy, toughness) through text alone, plus being able to identify your students' feelings from their writings, and deal with them appropriately. Start practicing writing this way now — by emailing your family and friends, for instance, or by signing up with an educational listserv and participating actively.

Consider using basic emoticons to add a primitive facial expression to your communications. Here are our favorites:

:)	basic smile
;)	wink
:-P	tongue out
:-D	big smile
:-(	frown

You are more than a teacher.

You will become more than a teacher to many; you will be a mentor, adviser, friend. Students will share personal problems, concerns, and questions with you, and in some cases, they may feel more comfortable sharing personal information than they would with a face-to-face teacher. You should be prepared. Allow this space for human interactions beyond the course material to flourish and revel in your new role.

Are you ready? Have you started to make notes in the Essential Checklist in Appendix C?

Essential Element 2: Build a course outline

Now is the time to examine the structure of your existing course or plan the structure of your new one. Whether you are building an online version of your face-to-face course, workshop, or corporate training session, or creating that new course you have been wanting to develop, the process is not terribly different. In each case, the starting point is an outline, which you will flesh out as fully as possible.

List your course objectives.

What do you want students to learn from your course? Most teachers have a set of learning objectives for their students, but in an onsite setting these objectives are not always written down or presented explicitly to students in a tangible form. In the absence of face-to-face communication, it is vital that you write down your learning objectives for the course and refer to them as you create each activity online. Be sure to avoid the use of jargon in your learning objectives, or, if necessary, consider two sets of objectives — one for the "review panel" and one for your real students to demonstrate what they've learned.

Develop an outline.

If you are converting an existing face-to-face course, this outline will likely mimic its current design, but you will adapt it over time to include the differences inherent in an online course. If you are creating an outline from scratch, see our insert box (see next page) to get started. Start by writing down all of your learning goals for your students, and then add a brief description of the lessons and activities that will enable them to achieve each of those goals. Use graphics or other concept

Consider the Following Questions
When Writing Your Outline

- What are your overall learning objectives for the students? What do you want students to learn and accomplish in your course? Center the content and activities of each week on at least one learning objective.

- What kind of material will you cover in the course? Outline the general flow of material that will be covered from the beginning to the end of the course.

- Consider learning cycles as you design the structure and flow of activities (e.g., hands-on activity, reading, discussion, assessment).

- What activities will help your students meet your learning objectives? Take the ideas you have brainstormed and break them out into individual activities for each week (or each module, or section). Skip the read-and-test routine and use group activities. Include offline as well as online activities. Insist on student-to-student interaction.

- Are there activities you would like to repeat from week to week, such as journal writing, weekly lab reports, or multiple visits to a specific website (such as an online newspaper with updated feature articles related to your subject matter)?

- Think about assessments. You will need to know if your students are "getting it," right? Will you use exams, quizzes, group work, papers, and/or final projects?

maps that allow your ideas to flow onto paper. Next, develop a rough timeline for the course, decide how much time to allot to each activity (see *Essential Element 12* for more information on pacing in an online course), and arrange the activities accordingly in your outline. Your outline will start with few details and then expand to include all activities.

Add bullets to your outline.

Once you have developed your basic outline, the goal is to create a "bulleted outline" in which each bullet point represents a separate document in your course — one for each activity and for each assessment. (See our insert box on the following page.) This means you will need to go through your outline multiple times, dividing multi-part activities into several bullets, one for each of its components. Think creatively about titles for course documents and use action verbs to make the titles descriptive and clear (e.g., "Ask a Question," "Meet Your Team," "Edit Your Short Story"). Aim to make your course outline complete now, detailing as many elements as you can to provide a rich and strong foundation on which you can add content later. You will use this bulleted outline as a reference to create your course documents.

Create a timeline for developing your course.

After you have drafted and redrafted your outline and have a good picture of what your online course will look like, you need to plan the development time of your course and include clear deadlines along the way. Don't underestimate the scope of this undertaking — preparing and designing your course is the most time-consuming component of the online teaching experience. It can require more development time than a face-to-face course because you must include step-by-step directions for each activity (from assigning specific page numbers in a book to directions on where and what to discuss in the reading; from including a link to a website to directions on what to do with the information on that website, etc.).

We have heard it told that you should allow at least as much time to develop your course as the amount of time needed to run the course. If that theory is correct, a one-semester course would require one semester to develop. Then there are those who have told us that double that estimate was just barely enough. There are too many variables to say definitively, since not everyone takes to learning a new technology at the same rate (and not everyone has the same amount of technical support available to them). Other factors include the length of your

Sample Bulleted Outline

Week 1: Meet Each Other
- Overview of Week 1
- Netiquette
- Ask a Question
- Meet Each Other — Part I
- Meet Each Other — Part II
- Just Hanging Out — Introducing the Water Cooler
- Logo Contest — Optional

Week 2: Build Community
- Overview of Week 2
- Tips on Managing Discussion Board Activities
- Build a Netcourse Community
- Edit Your Homepage
- Compose and Post Your Course Outline — 1 of 2
- Meet Your Support Group
- Create an Annotated Bibliography — 1 of 3
- Visit Your Private Space for Your First Evaluation

Week 3: Collaborative Learning
- Overview of Week 3
- Let's Talk
- Build Learning Communities
- Homepage Scavenger Hunt
- Create an Annotated Bibliography — 2 of 3
- Feedback Forum

Week 4: Introduction to Moderating
- Overview of Week 4
- Let's Talk
- Moderating First Hand
- Book Club — Learn to Moderate
- Create an Annotated Bibliography — 3 of 3
- Edit Your Course Outline — 2 of 2

course; how much multimedia, special plug-ins, or software you plan to use; how many online resources you've already identified; and whether you will be developing your course full-time, or if you have another job to attend to, too! Not only that, but not everyone can design creative activities within the same timetable, and there is no predicting how quickly someone can translate the knowledge they hold in their head, have it flow out their fingers, and appear on the screen in a decipherable and engaging course.

As you develop and expand your outline, and begin to create your course documents, keep careful watch on how much time you are spending, and either adjust your delivery date, your rate of creation, or the amount of assistance you need to match the demands of reality. If others will need to be involved to put your course online, check the schedule with them. Is it doable? As with everything related to technology, double or even triple your time estimate — you'll be glad you did.

Keep your start date in mind.

Perhaps you don't have a choice in the matter, and the date you are to begin offering your course is already determined. That makes it rather easy to set the timeline, even though preparing your course may take more time than you are allowed. If this is the case, the scope of the task may be of such a degree that you won't have the latter parts of the course completed by the time your course first opens. This surely is not an ideal situation, but it can and has happened. If this becomes your situation, you will want to be aware of how much slower course development progresses once you begin teaching. The new environment will take a good deal of your attention as you acclimate yourself to it, so squeezing in the final activities and content could become challenging if you have a full load of other courses to teach simultaneously.

Plan time to convert a face-to-face course.

If you are converting a face-to-face course to an online version, the process should, in theory, be considerably quicker than creating a new course you have never taught before. However, don't make the assumption that converting a course will be a quick and simple task. Your face-to-face course will require a good deal of modification to make it a success in an online environment. If you teach face-to-face, it's likely that much of your course lives "in your head," and is delivered to your students in the form of in-person lectures or discussions. You will need to create electronic versions of those materials. Add to that the adjustments you will need to make to activities, plus the many lines of instruction that are required, and the need for adequate preparation time starts to mount.

Plan (more) time to create a new course.

If you are not converting an existing course, but are beginning anew, read the tip above, then add to that time for creating the many interesting activities you will design, plus identifying or writing all the new resources you will need to go along with them. Also factor in time for researching online readings, websites, or animations to complement your course content.

Essential Element 3: Create a course schedule with clear deadlines.

Thinking about a schedule and timeline for your course goes hand in hand with creating a coherent course outline. Consider the following questions and issues as you plan the general flow of your course and expand your outline.

Choose your basic time unit.

What sort of work schedule and due dates will you have? We recommend dividing the outline and the course into weeks, thus providing a familiar and predictable time framework for your students. You might also choose to divide your course into modules, if there is a certain time frame associated with each module (anywhere from one to three weeks long).

In a scheduled, asynchronous course, students all engage with the same course material over the course of a week, but hand in work and contribute to discussions at times of the week that are most convenient to them.

- If you use a weekly time frame, make all assignments due by the end of the week.

- If you use modules, plan on due dates or weekly check-in points at the least, so that students are not left on their own for too long.

In general, it is best to avoid daily due dates, as some students may not be able to come to class daily.

Decide when your weeks begin and end.

Because your asynchronous online course is available 24/7 to students (and to you, the instructor), you will need to set arbitrary weekly time frames. Rather than starting on a typical Monday morning "work week," consider a Wednesday-to-Tuesday schedule, instead. There are a number of reasons why this schedule works better than a typical calendar week. For one, you, as the instructor, will not need to work Sunday evenings to post the new week's announcements, lessons, or starter discussion threads (save those till Tuesday afternoon or evening, instead). Second, students with busy schedules can work over the weekends (which will be mid-week of the course), without always feeling like they are catching up or coming in on the end of a conversation. Finally, students on a typical calendar schedule (Sunday-Saturday) won't miss an entire week of your class if they take a week-long holiday. In post-course surveys, online students have repeatedly voted in favor of the Wednesday-to-Tuesday schedule.

Determine the length of your course.

When deciding on your course timeline, factor in the following considerations:

- Plan for additional orientation time for your students to get comfortable with the technology and to get acquainted with each other.

- Keep in mind that the same activities from a face-to-face course will need to be spread out over a longer period of time in an online course.

- Remember that the same activity may take longer for students on a slower Internet connection, and that your students may have widely varying schedules.

Once you have decided on the length of the course, we recommend you look in a calendar and plan to schedule a week-long break around any major holiday periods, if possible.

Plan the workload.

Decide how many hours per week students will be expected to spend on your class, then design and place the activities accordingly. We recommend designing your course around an expected student time commitment of anywhere between five to seven hours a week, up to 10 to 15 hours per week, depending on the level of the class and the number of credits assigned. Your estimate should include the time needed for students to complete both online and offline activities, and you should aim to keep the workload even throughout the course, although it should be noticeably lighter at the very beginning. We believe five hours per week is the minimum amount of time in which students can still engage meaningfully with the course material and their fellow students.

Don't count technical time.

Whatever time frame you decide on, it should not include the time it takes for students to turn on their computers, log on to the course homepage, and wait for screens to display. Nor should it take into account the inevitable technical problems that will occur — your flexibility will account for that. ;-)

Think about the pace.

As you start putting weeks (or modules) into your outline, it is important to keep in mind that the pace of online asynchronous courses differs from the pace of onsite courses. Reading through many lessons and discussion messages online can be time-consuming for your students. Take account of this by planning time so that the pace of your course is consistent with online time demands (see *Essential Element 12*).

What's the critical mass?

Do you already know how many students will take your course, or are you going to advertise like crazy and hope for the best? Do you already have an ideal class size in mind? We recommend at least 12 students as a critical mass for producing quality discussions, with an ideal class size being somewhere between 12 and 25 students sharing the same discussion space. We've had successful courses with as few as 8 participants and as many as 28. If your course gets much larger than that upper limit, consider breaking it into two separate sections that run simultaneously, or one following the other. You will want to think about class size now, because the projected enrollment size will affect your design of group activities and class discussions. Consider also that it's not unusual for one or two students to drop the course before the course begins or in the early weeks, so you may like to over-enroll by a couple students to guarantee your target enrollment number.

Will you have synchronous meetings? Or not?

Will the course be completely asynchronous or will it contain some synchronous elements, such as live chat or even meetings in person? As with scheduling an onsite learning session, you will need to consider your students' schedules. Will they all be available and able to attend a synchronous event? If synchronous meetings and activities will be mandatory, be sure to alert prospective students to the time requirement in the course prerequisites.

If you do use chats, here are a few suggestions to make them more accommodating:

- Use them mainly as an efficient way of coming to decisions or answering questions, not for discussions you want to take deeper.

- If the courseware doesn't provide one automatically, save and publish a transcript for record-keeping purposes and for classmates who couldn't be there live.

- Insist on respectful references to others in the class, including those who may not be present.

- Schedule chats and office hours on different days of the week and different times to increase chances that more people can attend.

- Advertise your chat schedules well in advance, perhaps surveying what times will suit the most students.

- Provide alternative asynchronous solutions for students whose schedules prevent them from attending the offered live sessions.

Just as a face-to-face course can have some online components, an online course can also have some face-to-face components. It's up to you to decide whether you will run a completely online course, or include certain face-to-face elements such as local study groups, onsite training sessions, in-person office hours, or traveling/onsite technical support. It is important to think about this before you begin converting your course, since it will be affected by the following considerations: Do you have the budget to cover travel expenses? Do you have enough staff and monetary resources to host a meeting or training session in person? How will you handle students who are not able to attend these sessions?

What About Synchronous Chats?

Pros

- Chats allow a quick response time, which is good when you or students need an immediate answer or decision.

- They are good for quick communication between two people, like two co-instructors or two teammates, and can be used to quickly decide issues.

- They are useful as an "office hours" forum for scheduled private meetings and help sessions.

- They are good for group-brainstorming sessions, where everyone tosses out ideas.

- Some will allow application sharing for live visual technical help across distances.

Cons

- There's often no organized record of work and comments that have been posted.

- They exclude students from the conversation who can't arrange to be there live.

- Different time zones mean that some students may be absent and excluded from conversations.

- Some younger students should not be in unmoderated chats for fear of inappropriate content.

- Since it is hard to monitor for inappropriate content, strict supervision is required.

- More than just a few students present can make it hard for the instructor to find and respond to all questions.

- Technical and security issues or firewall obstacles can make it difficult to get everyone functioning.

- Discussions can be chaotic and fast, which makes it hard to engage in a solitary or few deep conversations and include everyone.

- Poor or slow typists are at a distinct disadvantage, often feeling ignored and excluded.

- Because it is easy to lose threads of conversation or interrupt others, it doesn't allow everyone to have a say.

- It is easy to get off track and distracted from the material at hand.

- It is harder to measure and grade participation.

OUACHITA TECHNICAL COLLEGE

- Location and scheduling: You may not wish to include face-to-face meetings if some of your students will be excluded due to their schedules or physical location. If you can find at least two students at each site, local study groups may work, but if not all students have this opportunity, you may choose not to use it.

- If you will be teaching to groups of students at the same location, we recommend a trained local "site coordinator" at every student site (see *Essential Element 5* for more information on site coordinators). This site coordinator acts as a liaison between the student and instructor or instructional institution. The site coordinator should be trained on the specific courseware being used, administrative issues, as well as general technical and computer-related skills.

Essential Element 4: Plan for ongoing quality assurance.

In a face-to-face course, you might have an anonymous suggestion box, pass out pre- and post-course surveys, and have an evaluator sit in on your course, or meet with other teachers and students to discuss ways to improve your course. All of these things can and, indeed, should also be done in your online course so you can receive candid feedback and improve your course over time.

Create standards.

Either alone, or with other online teaching colleagues, or an administrative team, create design and delivery standards for your course(s) that match the same minimum standards you have for your face-to-face courses. Make sure a procedure is in place that ensures regular evaluation of the course will take place during both the design and delivery stages. Is there a department or person in charge of evaluating your onsite course? Are they also responsible for evaluating online courses?

Encourage student feedback.

Encourage student suggestions on the course design and delivery. Provide a virtual "suggestion box" for students to pass along suggestions while the course is in delivery. This might take the form of an anonymous survey (most courseware allows this). Create a survey in which you ask students for their thoughts on the course, and make a link to that survey accessible throughout the course. Let students know that they can provide anonymous feedback at any point through this mechanism. Then, create a table or spreadsheet where you can compile and categorize these suggestions and check them off when you have addressed them. If you don't document them as they come in, you are more likely to forget them.

Request anonymous evaluations.

Include post-course questionnaires for students to fill out anonymously (check the software specifications to see if this is possible) with their feedback and suggestions for improvement. If it is not technically possible to keep student feedback anonymous within the course, make your students aware of this fact. Or suggest an alternative anonymous form, perhaps standard "snail" mail.

Welcome a mentor or peer.

Consider inviting faculty advisors or mentors to assist or offer feedback during delivery of the course. Take advantage of the experience of other online educators; they can offer general insights into teaching online, as well as particular tips and tricks for the software you're using. Listen to their feedback on your teaching style; it will help you grow as an instructor.

Keep a journal of your online teaching experience.

Create teacher note documents where you record comments as well as ideas for revisions as the course is in progress. Time — including virtual time — flies. Don't assume you will remember some quirky thing you discovered about the technology in order to get the assessment you're using in week three to work, or the announcement you know you will want to write each session during week five. Make notes for yourself — about what works, what needs refining — as you are teaching. Include personal notes, too, about how you feel about teaching online. Remember, this is a learning experience for you, too. You will want to record it.

Host an open forum.

Create a discussion thread where students can reflect openly about how they feel the course is going for them. Encourage students to share their feelings about the materials and assignments, the pace of the course, and any frustrations or inspirations they've experienced. By reflecting and sharing these thoughts as a group, students can help each other resolve problems, while realizing that they are not alone in feeling a certain way. This type of informal self-assessment also provides a means for students to touch base with their feelings about online learning, and clues you in as to what's working in the design and delivery of your course and what's not.

Provide an end-of-course evaluation.

The purpose of this evaluation is to survey your students' feedback on their experiences in your course. You will use the responses to assess and improve your course, helping to ensure a rewarding experience for future students. Try to make the questions specific and brief, though you will also want to include ample opportunities for open-ended feedback.

Among the many topics you might have in mind, consider these topics for inclusion in your evaluation:

- How well did your students feel they reached the posted learning objectives?
- What were the most rewarding and the most unsatisfying aspects of their experiences in the course?
- How would they rate the course materials you used?
- How adequate did they feel your feedback and evaluations were?
- Would they recommend the course to others and, if so, what preparation would they advise?
- What readings, resources, or activities, if any, would they like to see added or removed from the course?

Also, check with your department head or supervisor of online courses to see if there are questions that should be included in each end-of-course evaluation, to compare online courses within a program, or to compare online courses with existing face-to-face courses.

Essential Element 5: Ensure support from your administration.

Just as it takes a village to raise a child, it takes an administrative team to offer an online course. Your school or organization needs a strong administrative support structure to deal with marketing, registration and tuition, policies and procedures, and ongoing professional development for online teachers.

It takes a team to offer online courses.

Despite the fact that you are, of course, wildly capable of all manner of things, we want to warn you against assuming that you alone can provide all the services for your course. Designing and teaching your course will keep you plenty busy, so it's best if there are support staff to handle your administrative needs. Even if your school or organization is offering only a single course — yours — it will take a diverse team of individuals to make that course function smoothly. But don't fret if you are a small school or company — you don't need to devote anyone full-time to this effort. As the number of courses and students increases, the number of team members will grow, too.

Develop policies and procedures.

Policies and procedures help to keep schools — whether brick and mortar or virtual — functioning smoothly. Be sure there are policies that address your concerns for online teaching and learning. Involve staff members who will be affected by the policies, as they will accept them more readily if they are consulted during the development stage and because a diverse group will bring a greater number of ideas to the table. Your school or institution should advertise the new policies, preferably online or in any area easy to reference.

Provide organizational services.

- **Advertisement and recruitment.** Unless you have a captive audience, your courses will need to be marketed, which requires marketing personnel. The guidance department often serves this role in the school setting. Depending on your situation, the courses may be added to existing course catalogs, advertised locally or via newsgroups, or through a company newsletter.

- **Registration.** If you teach at a school, the existing registrar (and staff they might employ) might be the logical person, or team, to handle all registrations for your course, as well. It is possible that the registration process will differ for online courses. Will the registrations be by phone or mail, or will they be electronic? If the options for students include registering via your website, it is important to include the technical staff in planning and implementation. Your registrar and staff will likely need information and training on how to handle the new process. If you are in an organization without a registrar, who will handle this important task? Who will set up the system if there isn't one already in place?

- **Tuition collection.** If your organization or school doesn't already collect tuition for courses, a process will need to be developed if your online course will be offered for a fee. Does your courseware provide for it? If not, who will handle this process?

- **Supplying materials.** Online courses invariably need physical supplies, such as software, books, paper handouts, CDs, lab kits, and videos (see *Essential Element 9*). You will need to decide if you will provide these materials to students, or if they will be responsible for getting the materials themselves. If you go with the former, then you will need to set aside time and funds to order, distribute, and maintain inventories, or find someone in your organization who can handle these important tasks.

- **Teaching assistance.** If you are carrying a heavy load of teaching several courses and providing other services, you might benefit from an assistant to help you. Perhaps an assistant could alert you to absentee students, notice when someone is not completing assignments satisfactorily, help grade students' work, or provide technical assistance. This is a good way for prospective online teachers to learn about the process, the courseware, and the requirements of teaching online, and help prepare them for developing and teaching their own online courses later.

- **Administrator.** You may find that you need someone to help with administrative duties, someone who can free up course development and teaching time for you. If you have a teaching assistant, perhaps that person can help email participants, create course lists, send out announcements and warnings, make decisions about policies and changes, print certificates of completion, and report grades.

- **Course content support.** To assure consistent and high-quality content for your courses, it is helpful to have someone responsible for locating new resources and updating old ones. This includes double-checking the content, and proofreading for inconsistencies and appropriateness. In addition, courses can be improved by incorporating feedback and suggestions into course revisions, and making sure language is current.

Provide adequate staffing support for course-builders, teachers, and students.

It is essential that everyone involved in the actual course building and teaching of online courses has adequate technical support. Teachers and course-builders (if different from teachers) need access to knowledgeable help as they develop and teach their courses. It is important that specific staff are available to provide the right answers and support, and that they will be there when called upon.

- **Training.** Some users may be able to learn the courseware independently, but that certainly won't apply to all. Plan for training — plus ongoing technical support — on the courseware and any required software.

- **System administration.** The system administrator(s) should oversee the courseware, as well as the web server that your course resides on. In addition, they or someone else will likely create and maintain a website that offers your courses and related services to students and visitors. System administrators may be the best people to offer technical training to the staff who need it, as well as technical support to teacher and students.

Between semesters or terms of your course offerings, there are a variety of technical activities that require attention. These activities include removing student access when courses close, changing course dates and due dates, archiving courses, copying courses, and entering student names in preparation of starting a new run. These are tasks that would logically fall to the technical staff, but you and they may decide, together, that it is up to you.

- **Student support.** Students in online courses can easily feel adrift without the familiar situation of having a teacher and classmates they can see. Guard against this tendency by providing methods of comforting students, either electronically and/or in person. Consider providing virtual "hand holding" support, and keep in mind that you may be able to offer onsite support, as well. Local study groups in which several students get together for discussion, watch a video, participate in a role play or lab experiment are another way to offer in-person support to online students. Students who have been members of a local study group often report gaining extra comfort and confidence from this team.

- **Site Coordinator.** If several of your students are from the same educational institution, the best method for supporting them is to provide a site coordinator. This is a very important person at the brick and mortar location who is assigned to serve as a liaison between students and teachers, administrators, guidance counselors, and parents, if applicable. Site coordinators can also serve as technical consultants, if they possess the knowledge and skills to handle and solve technology problems. Their administrative tasks might also include scheduling computer access, recording grades, finding answers for all student questions, and making sure students are going to class.

Site coordinators can be among the most influential members of online course teams, which means that they not only need training in order to perform their job as required, but also need easy access to those who can help them provide the many services that students will ask of them. Keep in mind that each physical location needs its own site coordinator.

Develop and enforce course standards and quality control.

Standards help to ensure that courses are quality courses, both in terms of content and delivery. Even if your school or organization offers only your course, they will want to create standards that every course should meet. We suggest these include separate sets of standards for design and delivery. These standards may also have to take into consideration and work within existing local, state, or federal frameworks.

Keep your standards up to date, soliciting feedback from a body of advisors, evaluators, and from online students. Schedule course evaluations during course development, during delivery, and after any significant course modifications are made.

Provide ongoing professional development.

Once you are actively involved in online teaching, there is a powerful opportunity for learning and sharing ideas with others by taking advanced online courses, and by joining online communities or discussion forums.

Essential Element 6: Provide technical support.

One of the biggest differences between onsite and online courses is that the latter are highly dependent on technology. This means that students and teachers will need a minimum amount of technology literacy, a willingness to experiment with technology and problem solve when things don't go right, and lots of patience. Many of the issues covered in this section don't come up at all in face-to-face courses, so you'll want to be on the lookout and make sure you have adequately addressed them before your course begins.

Start with yourself.

Educate yourself on how the courseware works, and learn about its capabilities, features, limitations, and bugs. Practice using the courseware from the perspective of both a designer and a student. You might seriously consider taking a course on how to use the courseware, or arrange for training from someone knowledgeable onsite. Make sure you have plenty of time to experiment with it before your timeline requires you to put your course together. (*Hint:* Create a "play" course where you can practice different courseware features. For instance, if you want to post a survey, do it first in your play course; then when you have learned how it works or what variations (workarounds) are necessary to make it work for you, you will be able to do it right the first time in your real course.)

Practice patience in the face of (technological) adversity.

Technology problems will happen — that's just a part of the computer world (bummer!). You will need patience and creativity when faced with technology problems, as well as an eagerness to experiment, take risks, and play with new software. In other words, you should not be afraid to click a button. Practice patience with the technical team, too. Keep in mind that, in most cases (although not necessarily all!), the technical folks did not cause the technical problem you are experiencing — although it *is* easy to point fingers in that general direction when the technology goes amiss. Hold off on that reaction, and let the technical team help you instead. After all, that's their job!

Know your audience.

How comfortable is your audience with using technology? What kinds of computers and Internet connections can you expect them to have? If there are must-have or must-do technical prerequisites for your course, advertise them so your students know what to expect (see *Essential Element 14*). There is no reason that students with little technical background should not succeed in your course — as long as you inform them of what they need to know ahead of time (sometimes it's as simple as having some web experience or knowing how to use email). Provide a technical orientation, and always give clear instructions. Even the technically savvy will benefit from clear and detailed instruction, especially if the delivery software is new to them.

Walk in a student's shoes.

Make sure you experience your course using the minimum connection speed you advertise as acceptable for your students, so you're sure it is doable at that level. If you are accustomed to working on a T1 line at the office, for example, but tell students that a 56K connection is workable, use one yourself, to be sure the course functions adequately at that speed. What frustrations do you have with the modem? Are there any limitations you hadn't considered? How much longer does it take to read a sample discussion thread at this connection speed? Do all the course images load properly? Have you checked all other multimedia?

Give good directions — Part I.

At the beginning of your course, describe to students how to get around in your virtual space. Think of your course as your house and give them a tour. Even if your students have been in other virtual "houses" (courses), they don't know yours. Let them know everything — but be organized. One document can describe all the navigational buttons, for instance. Use another to describe technical terms students may need to know.

Another option to consider is using a formal orientation course, perhaps a mini self-paced course you make available just before your course starts. This orientation could be used across all institutional courses. The courseware you choose may also provide an orientation, but you will need to point students to it and ask them to complete it before beginning your course. Of course, you would want to take such an orientation yourself, too, to both learn what you can and to assess how valuable it could be to your students.

Give good directions — Part II.

Instructions for completing assignments and technical instructions must be written clearly at a very basic level, and either be repeated frequently or be easily located and advertised whenever needed. We cannot stress enough how crucial this is for the success of your course. Students may have a limited experience with either the courseware or the web in general, and feel great intimidation in your course. They need to be instructed, step-by-step, how to perform each segment of an assignment. Remember how overwhelming the first online course can feel, and keep those feelings in mind as you create clear directions in your course.

Give good directions — Part III.

At the bottom of each document, provide instructions for what to do, or where to go next. Especially at the beginning of the course, you will want to let students know exactly what to click when, and how to navigate in your course. For example, you might include screenshots of the appropriate buttons or links students will use. As the course progresses, you may decide to decrease your use of these navigational reminders, if the structure of your course is consistent and obvious. (There is, however, little harm in keeping the reminders throughout the course; they can continue to aid students, long after you thought them unnecessary.)

Make time for learning the technology.

Build in time for students to learn the technology at the beginning of the course. Create opportunities for students to practice technical techniques they will need to know for future graded assignments. For instance, some courseware offers specialized ways for students to "hand in" their more formal homework by adding attachments to discussion documents, creating a unique kind of document or "work assignment," or uploading documents to the course web server via a "drop box." Allow the students to do at least one trial run before the real deadline for the first big assignment, when a technical glitch could cause them to be late with their homework.

Don't use technology just because you can.

You don't want to make your course so high tech that students have numerous and ongoing technical problems; therefore, avoid flashy technologies unless they add to the course content and objectives. If you decide to use technologies that require special software or plug-ins, be sure to advertise what they are in your pre-course description (see *Essential Element 14*). Keep in mind that you may need to provide extra technical help with these plug-ins or software during the course.

Don't use the courseware's capabilities just because they exist.

Instead, use only what you need and what helps your students learn. Courseware is designed with lots of different users in mind, and consequently has lots of features available. You should be familiar with them all (or as many as possible) ahead of time, but you should not feel obliged to use them just because they are there. Think simplicity of form: Use what you need to accomplish your goals. Bells and whistles aren't always necessary.

Use the courseware features to best suit your needs.

A software designer created the courseware you are going to use, but you may decide that you will disable certain features or use them differently than described, depending on your unique audience and the course you want to deliver to them. Go for it. Just be sure to tell your students exactly what they are looking at, and how to make the courseware work for them, too. And consider letting the courseware designers or, perhaps, a larger newsgroup of users know how you are using the software. They will appreciate your feedback, and may even design certain features with you and your audience in mind next time around.

Provide technical support for your students.

Despite all the careful directions and the technical orientation you provide, your students will likely have many technical questions. Plan for that eventuality and provide a reliable method for students to get their technical and navigational questions answered, whether by you or by someone else knowledgeable in the technology. First, decide how you will offer solutions to your students. Is there a staff person in your organization who will provide this service? If so, find out now and make friends with this person or team. You'll be glad to have them on your side! Or will you be the sole person responsible for getting your students the technical help they need? Will problems be reported and/or remedied within the course? On a designated web page? By phone or email?

Advertise how to get help.

Your course *will* have technical problems (did we already mention this?), and students with even small problems need to be tended to quickly and surely. It is essential to provide immediate and accurate technical support for all problems your students encounter, and it is up to you to communicate clearly to your students how they go about reporting their problems. We recommend devoting a special thread in the discussion area strictly for technical questions and letting students know that they should ask all their questions there. Otherwise, their questions can get mixed in with content threads and go unnoticed for longer than wanted.

Make it visible.

Make all technical communications and problem solving visible to the entire class so everyone can learn from them. Students may be tempted to ask their technical questions privately (in email, on the phone, or in a private discussion thread within the course) because they are embarrassed by their lack of knowledge. Encourage students to ask all technical questions in the public sphere by reminding them that if they have a question, so do at least three others in the class, who will immediately worship them for being the first to ask.

Consider a technical FAQ document.

You will find that there are repeat questions that a number of students have. Can you anticipate some of these ahead of time and create a "Frequently Asked Questions" document? Add to this list over time, as you get a feel for the most frequent questions that students ask.

Section 2:
Design Your Online Course

You've prepared yourself and planned your course outline. Now it's time to begin designing your course. Do you have a face-to-face course you will convert to an online offering, or will you be developing a brand-new, never-before-offered course? The process is the same in either case and, in fact, is quite easy — *as long as* you realize there are a number of *Essential Elements* to keep in mind while you are putting together your course. Although an online course shares many similarities with a face-to-face course, it also has many differences that require special attention in order to guarantee success in its delivery.

In this section, we walk you through the essential design elements that allow your students to focus on the content, build a rich and engaging online community, learn from varied and meaningful course materials, enjoy inspiring individual and group activities, and do it all in the time allotted. It is up to you, the course-builder, to design your course so these wonderful learning opportunities can occur, and we will lead you through that structuring process.

Essential Element 7: Format your course so that students can focus on the content.

You are anxious to put your course on the web, right? Ready to create web pages that convey your personal style, as well as the information you need to get across to students? This is the fun part — but it also involves certain design tips, which we share here. It is not just about web pages looking nice; design is important for effective learning, too.

Create document templates.

Once your outline is complete, and you are ready to begin creating course documents, consider structuring your course by creating templates for your content. Make a template for each of the different types of documents you will use in your course. This will not only make your documents consistent and clear to students, it can save you a tremendous amount of development time. Spend time early on designing documents that have a sensible structure: an overview statement, list of learning goals, set of instructions, and memorable and recognizable graphical clues, among others.

You will likely have several standard document types. These may include:

- overviews;
- assignments;
- group activities;
- readings;
- journal work; or
- repeating lessons (such as a "Book Club" or "Weekly Check-in," for example).

Templates can exist as word processed documents or in HTML format, depending on your ultimate method of conversion for the courseware. Templates make for design efficiency: You can simply "plug in" information for each section of the document. They also make the course web pages predictable for students, so that, for instance, students know they will find the learning objectives in a bulleted list at the top of the document and the expectations for that assignment at the bottom.

You will also control the overall look and length of your documents if you stick to a template. (Of course, you shouldn't be too rigid. Allow yourself the freedom to design other documents, outside the traditional "template" look. Be consistent *and* be creative.)

Use clip art where appropriate.

Graphics add color, variety, clues to the subject, and eye-pleasing "white space" (around the graphic, that is) to a web page. Graphics should be related to the text, and not simply act as "fluff" or filler. They should not require too much disk space, as that could affect the web page loading time, especially for those on a slower Internet connection. Repeated graphics — based on a consistent theme — can be used to signify content that reappears often in your course (expectations or learning objectives, for example). For instance, we often use a set of apple icons to mark the "Expectations" section, which is always located at the bottom of each assignment document.

EXPECTATIONS

- You're expected to make one posting in the Discussion Board for this assignment. In the next assignment, you'll make additional postings to this thread.

- Always let us know **immediately** if your iguana ate your computer or if there are other circumstances that interfere with your ability to make a required posting.

Let your personality shine.

In your face-to-face course, you might tell jokes or have lots of great posters on the wall. Why not include cartoons and interesting graphics in your lessons to achieve the same effect online? People who haven't experienced an online course worry that the human element is lost, but a great deal of your personality and the ambiance you want to convey can be expressed online through the use of graphics and multimedia, such as animation, video, audio, etc. Use puns, titles, and graphics that build on your course themes and subject matter.

Use animations sparingly.

Use animation, video, or audio only if it improves the course material and not as a gimmick. Use multimedia to demonstrate concepts you normally demonstrate visually or "hands-on." Note that the production time for creating some Flash or other animations can be quite long and the process expensive, so plan and budget for it. Verify in advance that all your students are able to access the multimedia, or don't use it. Keep in mind also that your online course doesn't need to be completely online and, therefore, does not require fancy animations or simulations; students can still do "hands-on" activities on their own, locally.

Adopt a consistent, sensible layout for all your documents.

Your approach might include these examples:

- Choose readable typefaces, and avoid using too many fonts (use a maximum of two or three).

- Stick to plain black text on a light background, except special effects here and there.

- Special effects should be used sparingly.

- Avoid overly large fonts that waste valuable real estate, or very small fonts that are too small to read (*Note:* students' browsers can override your choices).

- Use only relevant graphics, and keep the file sizes as small as possible.

- Use bullets (like this one) or numbered lists in place of wordy paragraphs.

- Reserve underlining of text exclusively for web links.

- Use more "white space" than you would for a printed document; and

- Test your course documents with your monitor set to an 800 × 600 pixel size, to verify that students with this basic monitor limitation find that your documents are readable, and adequately fit their screens.

Keep it generic? Or personalize?

Who is your audience? Will this course be tailored to a specific audience or does it need to be versatile enough to be delivered to a variety of different audiences? Since the lessons will be in written form (much more so than in a face-to-face course), you will need to think about how you address the audience through your writing before you begin. If the audience changes, how easy will it be to customize the language of your lessons? It is unlikely that you would offer the same course content to fifth graders and to adults, so you may not have to worry too much about the type and level of language you use. On the other hand, what if you have a specific group of students for one session — say, a corporate client — but expect students from several different organizations in following sessions? To avoid rewriting between class runs, you may like to save much of the individualization of the course for the announcements area or the discussion threads.

Converting is not just transferring materials.

If you have a face-to-face course that you are now putting online, do not assume you can just transfer your activities and materials straight from your original course to an online course. Your activities will need a different type of student-to-student interactivity, and your text materials may be too wordy. They may need condensing into a different format (see *Essential Element 10* for more information on converting existing face-to-face activities).

Essential Element 8: Design a learning community that is collaborative, engaging, and inclusive.

A community is a necessary and integral part of a functional learning group. Students need to bond in a community in order to have a sense of trust with each other and respect for each other's ideas. With this level of common trust and value — so that students openly share their thoughts and feelings with each other and respect the viewpoints of their peers — students construct knowledge together as a group. This is where real learning happens.

Achieving a strong community doesn't just happen, however; instructors need to build in the structure and activities to offer this "coming together" opportunity to the students. Here, we explore ways to help build community online. Many of the strategies are those you probably already know and use face-to-face in class or workshops, so you can transfer your knowledge from that familiar context into this new one.

First, build trust.

As the instructor, be a role model. From the beginning of your course (and even before that in the pre-course materials you send out), set the tone for a trusting environment. Start by stating your rules for netiquette, including showing respect for each individual in the course and using appropriate tones in your communications.

State the community expectations.

Communities function best when the expectations and outcomes for community involvement are stated up front. If your students understand that you expect, and, in fact, require them to become acquainted; that you will provide opportunities for them to learn details about each other; and that you expect them to become members of friendly groups, then they will be prepared to follow through with those expectations.

Put communication first.

Interactions are an important part of the learning process and the process of getting to know one another, and thereby coming to trust one another. Structure course activities to be communication-centered — peer-to-peer and peer-to-group, and not just student-to-teacher (as in an activity that requires students to read material, write a report, and then send their homework to you). The more you build in opportunities for students to share with each other, the more they will be able to reveal about themselves, helping to build mutual trust and respect.

Start off on the right foot.

If you build relationships in the beginning of a course, the group work will prosper. If you don't build a community, individuals will feel out of it, lost, and unwanted. Build in extra time at the beginning of the course for orientation and settling in, and for students to get to know each other. This will take longer online than in a course with participants in the same room, and needs your help to happen. The first week of the course should be light, with graded work put off until the second week.

Get acquainted.

Include an initial icebreaker activity for students to meet each other at the beginning of the course. If the course is short — no more than six weeks — you will want at least one icebreaker. If it is longer (semester-length), use two or more and make them different styles that will interest a variety of student personalities. A single occurrence, one-type community-building activity won't reach all students. Not everyone feels comfortable with icebreakers; they may feel too "touchy-feely" for some and turn folks off. Still, it is important to break that ice, so go ahead and get corny, if you like. Then try a more formal getting acquainted activity, so that everyone has the opportunity to participate, according to different comfort levels.

For the initial activity, you might have students post personal information about themselves — their professional and personal interests, hobbies, activities — then have them read about their classmates.

Add a follow-up activity where students have a chance to make comments and converse about their similarities.

Other ideas include:

- Enter information about yourself in your "profile" (or other personal homepage), then go on a "scavenger hunt" to find similarities between students.

- Introduce yourself through the eyes of your pet or house.

- Describe your three favorite things (e.g., movies, books, foods, places to visit).

- Play a virtual game of "Survivor," only this time, have people voted in (not out!), based on clues they reveal about themselves that would make them particularly helpful on such-and-such an island, desert, or other wild area (like a virtual classroom!).

- Invite the first (or last) person on the alphabetical list of students to go first in starting a story about online learning, then pass the baton to the next person, and so on. (*Note:* Allow at least two weeks for this activity, depending on the number of students.)

Do you use icebreakers in your onsite course? If so, can you adapt them to work online?

Continue to get personal.

One or two icebreakers are not enough to build a community! Continue to create opportunities for personal interactions throughout the entire course. See our next tip, for example.

Coffee klatch, anyone?

Include a water cooler, café, or other student hangout area for non-course-related discussions. In a brick and mortar school, community building happens before and after class, before the instructor shows up or after she leaves — out in the hall. Online, you have to create a similar space for social interactions. If you don't create a space for them, these social and personal communications will intrude on the "real" discussions, diluting them and making it harder for students to get back on track with the learning objectives and goals for a particular assignment.

You can use an asynchronous thread that is available throughout the course or, perhaps, a synchronous feature, like chat, that is always available for students to drop in and see who else is visiting. Use a fun, engaging title for this space — anything goes. You will need to tell students about this space, what it's for, and how to use it. Be sure to convey any rules you feel are important for your students, such as showing respect for fellow students at all times. Reserve the right to remove posts if they break this rule. Feel free to post to this space yourself. After all, *you are a part of the community, too.*

You are a part of the community, too.

Keep in mind that you are part of the community — and an important part. Be sure to introduce yourself, both in a welcome statement, and also by providing personal information about yourself when your students share information about themselves. Although you might consider asking younger students to include graphics of themselves, instead of photos, thus avoiding any insecurities about their appearance, be certain to include a photo of yourself. Some people feel a strong need to have a visual image of who the instructor is, and will benefit from you including one.

Tone it down.

It is important for the instructor to model but not to dominate. If the predominate voice is the instructor's, the other students' voices won't be what students hear. Do not be a go-between for your students — let them experience each other.

Introduce small group work when it's time.

Don't break off into small groups until the larger community has been established. It is critical to wait a bit before beginning small group work, which could divide the larger group unnecessarily into smaller teams that don't ever feel a connection to the whole. Be sure that you've had a chance to build the full community, through icebreakers and full-class discussions, for instance, and then you will be able to split into smaller groups without fear of fragmenting the whole.

Be sensitive to your students.

Be sensitive to different cultures and religions (e.g., don't pass out [real or virtual] Easter eggs when folks celebrate Passover). And if you use American slang, make sure to define it in the next sentence. The community in your course is based on a desire to learn together, not necessarily on a common background; you may have students from different backgrounds, cultures, religions, and ethnicities. Celebrate these students coming together in your course — their differences will only serve to improve the dialogue.

Essential Element 9: Find and use appropriate course materials and resources.

You have the awesome power and reach of the Internet at your fingertips in an online course, and you *should* take advantage of this. Here, we have you take stock of the materials you use in your face-to-face course or workshop, and decide what you will keep, what you will remove, and what you will need to change in order to build a course that takes the most advantage of the educational possibilities of an online setting. If you are building a brand-new course, you have a variety of options available to you. Read below about providing content-rich online and offline resource materials and other reference documents.

Just because a course is online, it doesn't mean all your materials have to be.

Don't be afraid to snail mail all those wonderful things you use in your face-to-face course — CD-ROMs, kits, books, inexpensive lab materials, and other resources — to students. With a little planning, there is no reason why you can't incorporate these same materials into your online course, if you wish. Of course, the trick is to decide which hard copy materials are definitely worth keeping, and which might be better replaced or supplemented by materials that can be found online. If possible, use both web-based and offline resources. If you can't afford to purchase materials, utilize the resources of local libraries, or add the list to the student prerequisite information you send out.

Find new online resources.

Set aside plenty of time for research and reading to find new online resources. Start with educational portals on the web where you might just find materials equal in quality to the ones you would otherwise mail to students or have them purchase. In fact, you may find the very same materials online — in electronic format, of course. Many teachers put lecture notes or other materials online free of charge for educational use. Haunt educational listservs or newsgroups where other teachers hang out to get recommendations for great educational resources on the web. (*Hint:* Ask a graduate assistant or other associate to help out with this research.)

Find it electronically and save a tree.

Scanning print material takes time and work, so before scanning in lots of print resources for use in your course, find out if the material is available from the publisher in electronic format, or if alternate resources already exist online. Check whether printed material you use face-to-face or excerpts from them are available on the web in a format that is legal to use in your course. For example, many literary classics are available for public use on the Internet, and most big newspapers and magazines now publish online editions for a small cost or free of charge. Some authors or publishers choose to publish sample chapters or the entire contents of their books online.

Get permission.

Make sure you get appropriate permission for each piece of copyrighted material you plan to use. In your note to the copyright owners, let them know about your course (include a syllabus), when it will be offered, how many students will be in it, as well as whether you plan to run the course again (for example, the following semester). If you can't get permission, don't use the material. The good news is that many authors and publishers are willing to let their materials be used free of charge for educational purposes. (*Hint:* Try the Copyright Clearance Center at http://www.copyright.com for one-stop permissions shopping.)

Consider lending materials.

If you want to send "media kits" to your students, but are on a limited budget, consider sending materials for free, provided students agree to return them to you at the end of the course. That way, you can reuse the materials for the next set of students and amortize their cost over time.

Be sure to mail materials in advance so students will have them before the lesson begins, and always verify that students have received them. If students will be required to mail the materials back after the course ends, make sure they understand this and have both your ad-

While replacing offline materials with online ones can save money and time, there are a few considerations you should keep in mind:

- Be wary of replacing a hard-copy resource with just one web resource. Web pages can change or disappear at the blink of an eye, so it is a good idea to find several alternate web resources for each topic you want to cover.

- All web resources will need to be checked each time you run the course, and you should always check links just before they go live. URLs change and your readings may have to change with them.

- It can be difficult to read long text documents on the computer screen, and your students may have limited printing possibilities, so you may wish to mail books and longer documents before the course starts, rather than ask students to read them online or print them out for offline reading.

- You should never use material that has been put on the web without the author's or publisher's permission, nor should you copy material from a website into your own course without permission.

- Just because something is on the web does not mean it is reliable. You must carefully evaluate each resource you find on the web for accuracy and integrity. Do some research to find out who has published the website, what their motives and possible biases are, whether the material is current and up to date, and if there are many typographical errors and/or grammatical mistakes, for instance. Evaluate each web resource as carefully as you would evaluate any print material for use in your course.

- Determine your budget for purchasing and mailing hard-copy materials to students who may be scattered over a great distance. This alone may prompt you to look for more resources out on the web.

- Find out whether your students will be able to afford purchasing items themselves and, if so, whether those materials will be available where they live.

- Compare the quality of the materials available hard copy vs. online, and then decide whether you will be able to mail packages to students at the start of each course run.

dress and the means to return the materials. Consider using an online database to keep track of each kit's whereabouts.

Reach out to different learners.

Remember as you compile your materials that your students will have a variety of different learning styles. Wherever possible, try to incorporate a variety of methods for communicating your information. You can assure your visual learners a greater chance of understanding by using a variety of graphical representations of the materials, and kinesthetic learners can best benefit by working with interactive tools to understand given content. There are different types of media, each of them with a different potential for supporting learning. Whether it's on-screen text, books, videotapes, audiotapes, online simulators, games, or creative software — all reasonable examples — do not limit your content to one method, and most certainly do not make it *all* text.

Gather first.

Gather your materials, but do not begin placing them into course documents until you have laid out your course in a detailed outline. Decide on the order, the categorization, and the timing before you begin adding content, or you might have to redo documents later.

Create a set of additional resource links.

Just as you would have a rich bibliography for your onsite students with additional resources for them to pursue for their extracurricular studies, so, too, should you build a terrific online bibliography. Check the URLs frequently and keep the web page of resources updated. There are new sites being added to the web daily. Consider asking students for their own favorite sites to add to this list.

Essential Element 10: Develop rich, relevant activities to support your learning objectives.

Since your course will be a series of student activities, you'll want to develop new activities for the online environment or transform your current face-to-face activities for use online. As you recall, student activities include everything from reading course documents to required books, from searching external websites to participating in dialogues, debates, or role-plays in discussion threads. Let's explore how to create and transform activities for use online.

Use a learning cycle.

Consider using a predictable learning cycle, such as introduction, lesson, activity, and discussion. This effective pattern can prepare students in advance for the next step in their learning experience, and should always culminate with sharing their learnings with their classmates.

Create weekly overviews.

In addition to the course syllabus — which is located in a separate section of the course devoted to informational materials — you should create weekly overviews that summarize the topics, major activities, learning objectives, student requirements, and grading information (see example on next page). The overview document should be the first assignment document listed each week, to give students a big picture of what is expected for the week and help them plan how they will accomplish each task. Consider including a checklist of required activities, along with the type of activities (reading vs. discussion, for instance), and a blank column for students to check when they've completed each lesson. Suggest that students print this document and tell them how to use it as a hard copy checklist to keep track of their progress.

Can they swallow it whole?

Make documents and activities into "bite-sized" pieces, rather than "meal-sized" chunks. An existing face-to-face course has lots of content, some of it written down, some of it in your head. The temptation is to move all the lecture notes into course documents. This just creates a textbook online, which is not even close to being an online course — at least not the type of online course we are advocating here. The challenge will be to organize ("chunk") your material into a series of interactive lessons that take advantage both of your students' ability to connect over great distances and of the vast resources available on the Internet.

You can't chew a whole meal in one bite, nor can you digest too much information at the same time. Limit what you say in any one document. A web page that has too much information will likely be skimmed over or — worse — altogether ignored. So, then, how big is a "bite-sized" piece? A simple rule is to limit web pages to not more than two or, at most, three printed pages.

✓ Checklist
You'll find an assignment checklist at the bottom of the Overview document each week. Past participants have found it helpful to print this handy little checklist to keep track of which assignments they've completed. Use it as you like.

Week Two	Assignment Type	Completed
Tips on Managing Discussion Board Activities	Reading	
Build a Netcourse Community	Reading and Discussion	
Edit Your Homepage	Homepage Activity	
Post Your First Draft — 1 of 2	Posting	
Meet Your Support Group	Reading	
Create an Annotated Bibliography — 1 of 3	Support Group Activity	
Visit Your Private Group Space for Feedback	Private Group Space Posting	

A single activity only, please.

Each assignment document should contain information and instructions for a single major activity. If you have a reading and a discussion assignment, plus a web search, and a collaborative project all in one week, be sure to create different documents for each. Separating them allows for students to see clearly what they need to complete. The web, as the name implies, is an interconnected place, but that doesn't mean it has to be jumbled or disorganized. It is critical that the web of lessons that make up your course is organized.

Recast each activity for the online context.

If you are converting a face-to-face course or training session, you'll want to examine each of your existing activities and determine what changes might be necessary to make them work well in the online environment. Do any aspects of the course's current form require students to work in person with materials, the teacher, or other students? If the activity is engaging and meets your learning objectives, try to think about ways to restructure the assignment so you can continue to use it. In other words, don't automatically ditch those fabulous face-to-face activities; instead, think about how you can modify them. If you are creating course activities from scratch, you will want to be sure they meet your course objectives and are doable online.

Detail, detail, detail.

Include extremely detailed instructions for how to complete each assignment. Pay special attention to technical instructions. Consider using bullets or numbered lists to help students complete each task, step by step. Suggest that students print out complicated technical instructions and have their hard copy alongside them as they're following the steps, one by one. Also, let students know how to open a new browser window, so they can have instructions on one window, while they are completing the assignment in the other. Your explicit instructions will help prevent students from losing time by misinterpreting your intentions. They'll spend time on the activity, instead.

Test your instructions.

Don't forget to test your instructions yourself and, better yet, have someone else test them. If a stranger can find their way around the site without calling you, you're all set! (*Hint:* If your courseware package has different access levels for teacher, student, and administrator, be sure to log into your course as a student while testing, to be sure you're seeing everything exactly as students will see it.)

What's the grade?

Students need to know what's expected of them for each activity. If there is no tangible "hand in" or posting requirement, let them know what you expect them to have learned from that lesson. Include a clear and detailed set of expectations and/or a grading rubric with each activity.

Make it personal.

Personalize each document to communicate a sense of your personality to the student. This allows both you and the students to become comfortable in communicating online. But beware of personalizing too much for a particular one-time audience, especially if you think the type of audience might change next time through — unless you are willing to

As you convert or develop activities ...

- Include a set of written learning objectives for your students, and explain how they meet one or more of the course objectives.

- Imagine yourself in your students' position, and consider how they would perform the activity you are considering.

- Keep your students' situations in mind. How can you accomplish the goals of your activity without introducing barriers to performing the required tasks?

- If the activity requires a lab or materials, consider how the students can use those at their own physical location, or other institutions in their area. For example, students may be able to go to a local school, community college, or business to do a hands-on experiment. Consider replacing labs with online simulations, where appropriate.

- What resources might students easily find at their disposal, and what limitations might the students encounter? Keep in mind that students may not have the same means and privileges; design to be inclusive.

- If the activity requires a partner or team, consider how they work together through dialogue, while each completes their portion of the activity at their own site. Design the activity with contingencies for students whose partners vanish into virtual space.

- If the activity requires that the partner be local, plan for students to work with an associate, colleague, or acquaintance. Let students know about this activity well in advance of any due date, so they can schedule necessary local meetings.

- If quick communication is necessary for an activity, consider alternative methods of communication (e.g., phone, synchronous chats, or instant messaging).

- Ask one or more colleagues to go through the activity, and get their feedback. Have them read the activity from their computer and imagine how they would accomplish it. What materials might they need? What difficulties would they encounter? How long would the process take them?

rewrite each document each time you teach the course. Feel free to use contractions, and to write in a friendly, informal way. These are not formal lecture notes you're putting up on the web for possible publication. These are your class notes; consider them personal correspondence with your students.

Variety is the spice of life.

Present the content in a variety of different formats, including web-based and offline activities. By taking advantage of different activities and formats (e.g., readings, simulations, laboratory exercises, essays, peer review and critiques, discussions, presentations, and offline activities), you will make the course more interesting and allow comprehension by those with different learning styles. Doing the same activity over and over for the duration of the course might be predictable, but it also may be boring. Mix it up. Tap into your students' multiple intelligences. Take advantage of opportunities for musical, visual, social, emotional, and environmental learning.

Repeat yourself.

Do include repeating activities. Perhaps you would like to use a student journal for reflection or a weekly "book club" feature? When used appropriately, these repeating activities can provide a sense of structure and "grounding" for each week, forming a sort of backbone to the course.

Plan activities that require student collaboration.

Instructors should require student-to-student interaction and collaboration by establishing frequent and ongoing discussions on assignments, asking for student reactions or peer feedback, and setting up group work. Insist on student-to-student interaction. In other words, avoid making the class one in which students simply "hand in" homework to the instructor. Make sure the technology you choose to deliver your course allows for as much student interaction as possible, which can happen, for example, in a discussion board, chat, whiteboards, among other places.

Advertise the due date.

Require deadlines to help keep students on task and to keep group work and discussions moving. Announce a clear due date on each assignment, to provide students with the ability to plan, manage their time, and complete assignments on time. Remind students frequently of upcoming assignments, due dates, and long-range activities.

Essential Element 11: Include a balanced mixture of individual and group learning activities.

When designing your course, keep your mind open to new possibilities. Some e-learning situations call for independent work, such as essays or exams based on content you have delivered over the web. However, most quality online courseware applications also allow for discussions and, therefore, the possibility of student interaction over great distances. Take advantage of this — and of the pedagogical power of group work — by providing a mixture of individual and group learning activities.

Individual activities

Private versus public.

Independent work doesn't have to be private. For each independent activity you assign, consider whether it makes sense for the work students hand in to be private or to be visible to their peers, depending on what your courseware allows. For example, a weekly journal entry might be private, while a report or presentation might be better shared with the entire class. Questions that have only a single correct answer (such as a math problem set) might be best accomplished privately, while responses to open-ended questions could be shared in a public space. Whenever possible, allow students to share the results of their independent work with their classmates for the purpose of feedback, comparison, and collaboration.

Handing in work.

In a face-to-face classroom, you can call on students to answer a question and verify that they have completed the work you've assigned. Online, you need to purposefully build a method into the structure of your course to confirm students have completed the work. Design activities that require students to make a written response, which will allow you to check and assess their work, whether formally (for a grade) or informally. Because students have easy access to a wealth of information on the "Information Superhighway," consider questions that require students to voice their opinions on an issue or synthesize information in a new way, rather than those that call for a predefined answer. Your learning objectives for each activity will influence the type of questions that are appropriate.

A little bit every week.

Time management is an important issue for online students, who may be unaccustomed to structuring their own time and working on projects at their own pace. Even more mature students who are accom-

---

Ideas For Independent Online Activities

Consider the following types of independent activities in your online course:

- Assigned readings and responses;
- Question sets and answers;
- Written work (research papers, plays, essays, lab reports, short stories, poems);
- Art work, music, photos and visual artwork, graphic design;
- Multimedia presentations (web pages, PowerPoint, Hyperstudio, video, animations);
- Journal entries;
- Lab work or field work;
- Interviews in the local community or over the web;
- Book reports/critiques;
- Personal portfolios of work;
- Online flashcards, games, or drills;
- Reflections and observations on the activities, content, topics, structure, and pace of the course;
- Scavenger hunt, web quests;
- Self-assessments; and
- Parts of a whole (e.g., have each student research a different aspect of the same topic and then combine their work into a whole class compilation).

---

plished in time management may not initially be able to transfer their skills to a new environment. To help your students beat a potential procrastination problem, avoid long-term assignments with one final due date. Instead, devise ways to check your students' progress along the way. For example, have students complete drafts of papers (which can then be self- or peer-edited, relieving you of that responsibility). Students can gauge their preparedness for an important test by taking independent self-assessments periodically.

Get off the computer.

Have students get offline for observational work, interviewing other students or professionals, going to a town meeting, or doing some star gazing (for an astronomy course!). Different students will do better with different kinds of activities, so be sure to give them a wide range of independent work experiences.

Provide prompt feedback.

Regular teacher feedback is always important in an online course, but even more so with independent work, where students will look solely to you for acknowledgment of their work. Be sure to provide timely and thoughtful acknowledgment of all independent work that is handed in.

Group activities

Achieve balance.

Are you stuck in a read-and-test routine? Mix it up by including group activities. Participating in individual as well as group learning activities will provide your students with a rich mixture of experiences. In everyday life, you work independently and with groups of friends, colleagues, or committees. In your course, strive to achieve a similar balance of different types of activities. This helps your students to grow into well-rounded individuals, and helps them experience the course content from multiple perspectives. In addition, communicating with classmates keeps students engaged in the material and helps combat feelings of isolation that can creep up in the online course room. Knowing that others are out there waiting, listening, and responding gives students one more reason to keep coming back to class!

Make it collaborative.

Group activities can be defined in many ways: from whole-class discussions, for example, to smaller team projects, where each team creates a report, prepares a presentation, takes part in a role play, or debates sides of an argument. The key to good online course design is to build in different types of group activities, allowing learners to collaborate with each other and to engage with the course material in a variety of ways. Assign at least one group discussion activity every week and plan several major team activities throughout your course. Students will get better and better at accomplishing group tasks each time they practice. Alternate small group activities with class-wide forums that renew the sense of the whole.

Divide activities into separate parts.

Divide complicated team activities into a series of smaller lessons and provide a clear timeline, due date, and grading rubric for each part of the larger activity. This affords students a clearer understanding of each part of the larger activity, and reduces the chance of students missing a crucial component. It also allows you the opportunity to check for completion of one stage of an activity before proceeding to the next stage, and ensures a better success rate for your students. Breaking a longer group activity into sections will also allow you time to jump in and intervene earlier if a group gets off task or isn't progressing.

Create supporting materials in advance.

There are several things you can do in advance to make group work run as smoothly as possible.

- Decide on and define any roles you will assign in each team (leader, recorder, and so forth).
- Create interesting team names — use colors, planets, or something relevant to your course material. For example, if it's a plant biology course, choose interesting plant names. If you decide on a theme ahead of time, you can find relevant puns, graphics, and websites to enhance the material and make the group assignments more interesting for students.

Group similar students together? Or not?

Decide on your grouping strategy. Will it be random? If so, create a blank table with the team names that you can pop your students' names into at the appropriate time. Or, are you going to group students based on personality, skill level, or experience? If this is the case, make sure you have designed ways to gather the information you'll need in order to create the teams (for instance, through a student survey, or simply by asking them to write about themselves).

Consider grouping team members according to common interest, or by subject matter, if appropriate to the activity. For example, if your group project focuses on a specific area (e.g., creating a webliography of related websites around a common theme), grouping students according to those interests helps students to bond quickly and relieves them of the task of finding a common interest around which they can work. Use a pre-assessment to check for interests and commonalties, but beware of grouping like students together if the assignment doesn't specifically require it. Such grouping can feel artificial, plus the members will miss out of the benefits that diversity of ideas can provide. As your experience grows, group students using several different approaches, in some cases based on interest, and other times mixing them up randomly.

How big is just right?

Decide on group sizes ahead of time. Will all groups have the same number of students? Do they need to be odd or even numbered for any particular reason? Discussions can be hard to keep up with in very large numbers, but work may suffer if just one or two students are absent from a very small team. Think about these issues in conjunction with your specific activity to decide what sizes make the most sense.

Consider groups slightly larger than in face-to-face work. We have found that four to five students online is an ideal group size. Pairing also works, but be sure to provide contingencies for either partner if the other doesn't show up in class during the assignment period. You might include some activities where you group students and assign roles, and others where they choose partners and decide upon roles themselves (the latter will require more time). Be ready to suggest new roles within a group if the current configuration is not ideal, and to give students the opportunity to have new experiences.

It is possible that individual students may be absent at some point during the team activity, especially if its multiple parts extend over a period of weeks. Design the project in such a way that the project can move forward without all team members present at all times. Draft alerts that you can send to students as soon as you sense they are missing, or that the group interaction is lagging. If you have these messages ready in advance, you can send them at the first sign of trouble. Alternatively, plan for these contingencies by assigning this as one of the tasks of the team leader, or let the members know ahead of time what to do if one or more team members are absent (for instance, they could proceed without that student's input and the student can rejoin at a later stage).

Once you have defined and assigned groups, inform members of the timing for the team activity, as well as any special roles they will play. That way, they can plan ahead and let you and their group know if they have any scheduling conflicts.

Include clear instructions.
- Give very specific and detailed instructions when assigning group learning activities. As in the onsite classroom, online teamwork is not necessarily easy, especially given that much formal education relies on independent work. To ensure that the team process is as successful as possible, make your written instructions clear and detailed.

- Explain that one of the most important tasks in any group project is for all members to learn how to work together as a team.

- Make it clear when the activity starts and stops.

- Include the who, what, where, when, why, and how in your instructions.

- Select and rotate team leaders for each week of the project, to give everyone a chance to experience the role, and to avoid the team's work suffering from a single inadequate leader.

- If there are additional individual roles for team members, describe them and your expectations for each.

- Provide detailed and clear student expectations for behavior on a team. These would likely include civility, support, kindness, gentle language, empathy, encouragement, regular attendance.

- Use visual illustrations and examples, along with written instructions to explain particularly complex instructions.

- Provide task checklists for your students to print and use off-screen.

Group work takes time. Allow for it.

- Introduce the concept of group work a few weeks before it is to begin, and announce its approach, which will help prepare students for what to expect.

- Allow ample time to complete the work, often a considerably longer time span than in face-to-face classes to account for the asynchronous scheduling. When you break into smaller groups, the members will need "getting acquainted" time, as did the larger class as a whole. Plan assigned activities for this process — and encourage it to happen.

- Consider whether or not you will create a private or public discussion area for each team. Would students benefit from a possible "cross-pollination" of ideas between teams or would the volume of team postings overwhelm other students?

- Check student schedules to avoid scheduling a team leader during a busy time.

- Consider using synchronous group events for accomplishing team introductions or, perhaps, for group decision making (see *Essential Element 3*).

- Acknowledge that group work can be hard to do online, but by accomplishing it, students are learning how to succeed in the real world where working on a team is a part of life.

When to use different groups.

Group work is not always easy; it can confound, frustrate, and ultimately fail (or at least produce less than a superb final product). Don't let that fact deter you, because, alternatively, group work can be extremely rewarding and the source of an inspirational work, unachievable by any individual alone. Over time, you will likely see both extremes of experiences in your course. Reserve the right to use different groups during the course, so that students have multiple experiences with group work and get to work with different people (different opportunities and experiences allow for different successes).

Ideas For Online Group Work

Consider the following types of group activities in your online course.

- Content-related discussions;
- Discussions of the results of students' individual research;
- Peer review and feedback of each other's posted work;
- Peer moderation of discussions;
- Debates;
- Simulations or role plays;
- Book critiques;
- Co-developed products (research paper, lab report, short story, web page, multimedia presentations, artwork, plays, stories); or
- Discussion of reflections and observations on the activities, content, topics, structure, pace of the course.

Flavor it international.

Take advantage of the fact that your course is online, connecting people with different backgrounds, perhaps across geographical regions. Can you expand your activity to include a more international focus? Could you have students contact peers around the world, compare and contrast local beliefs, customs, regional data? Talk to international experts or mentors? Participate in webquests with students from other schools?

Allow time to digest.

After each group activity, consider holding a debriefing session where students can talk about their experience, reflect on some of the challenges faced, and share success stories. This will allow them to think about ways they can improve group communication, and also give you ideas for new ways to structure future group activities in your course. Based on student feedback, for example, you might change a group project timeline, increase or reduce team sizes, or group students in a different manner.

Essential Element 12: Recognize that pacing in an online course is different.

As you start putting weeks into your outline, it is important to remember how the pace of online, asynchronous courses differs from onsite courses. In an onsite course, students are generally working on the same activity — whether that is listening to a lecture, discussing a reading in a seminar, or engaging in a group activity, such as a laboratory exercise. As the "bell rings," they transition to their next class or assignment. In an online class, students are working at different locales and at different paces. Consequently, they can be working on multiple projects at the same time. While they are waiting for responses from their colleagues on one assignment (for example, their reflections on a reading), they could also be conducting research, gathering materials, completing other online or offline reading, or participating in a discussion on a different topic. Overall, it takes approximately the same time to deliver content onsite as online; the difference is in the pacing.

Begin slowly.

Especially important is the beginning of the course, when everything is new to students. Build in time for students to learn the technology before starting to work. Have students practice in ungraded exercises all the technical techniques they will need to perform later for a grade. Also build in extra time for them to get to know each other. This will take longer online than in a face-to-face course, and needs your help to happen. (See *Essential Element 8* for ideas on getting acquainted.)

Let students get their feet wet first.

Devote the first week of the course largely to class orientation (more specific than the technical orientation to the courseware, this brief orientation document refers to *your* course, as opposed to how to use the courseware), technical overviews, and meeting fellow classmates. Students will be getting acquainted during this initial period and adjusting to the asynchronicity of your online course. This is an important week to set the tone for the rest of the course. Be gentle: Save the more intense activities for the weeks that follow.

Plan multiple activities.

Plan several activities around a similar topic for each week, so that students can multi-task and learn through different means. Work on multiple projects at the same time, to allow them to happen independently and simultaneously.

Schedule for asynchronicity.

Asynchronous means students get online throughout the week and perhaps in small chunks of time, as opposed to one extended period of time. Online activities, therefore, differ in pace from their face-to-face counterparts, where class sessions of one to three hours in length are more the norm. Additionally, the times that all students choose to get online will likely not match, so the time it takes to accomplish a certain goal (for example, a small group of students deciding on a format for their final presentation) will be longer than if all students were online at the same time.

Divide and conquer.

Divide complex, long-term assignments into small, single-topic portions, with multiple due dates and instructor checkpoints, to ensure students are engaged at each step, and are on-track and progressing. Design a deliverable — whether that's a minimum number of required postings or a draft of a final product — for each stage of the project.

Provide check-in points.

Don't give a long-range assignment without having a series of checks along the way (e.g., draft an outline, refine it, post it, have classmates comment on it, redraft, publish). Generally, if there is a way to procrastinate, students will do so. Said another way, if the whole project isn't due until it's due, it won't get done until then. For more complicated or longer assignments, provide interim deadlines, with expectations for each section.

Redefine due dates.

Students need to be made aware of the critical difference between a synchronous course that meets once per week and one that is available to them 24/7. In an online course, you can't allow your students to wait until the end of the scheduled week to post their work; if they do, that single posting will fall short of the required posting commitment, which insists that students log in to your course and post to the threaded discussion area throughout the week (on some minimum number of days which you will make clear in your Learning Support Agreement; see *Essential Element 14*). Without checking into the course frequently, students will miss the input from their colleagues' multiple postings that would serve to help expand their knowledge on the subject.

Essential Element 13: Provide equal accessibility to all students.

The issues surrounding accessibility are complex, complicated by the rapid changes in technology that affect website readability. Students of all abilities have the same rights to access online courses, and the burden is on course designers and course developers to work to ensure their courses provide equal access to all students, regardless of their abilities.

Don't worry: You don't have to become an expert on accessibility issues. There are several groups and organizations that provide information, resources, and tools to check the accessibility of your course (see our list of resources in Appendix A).

Follow the Web Content Accessibility Guidelines.

By following the Web Content Accessibility Guidelines, you can design your course to meet the needs of all your students, excluding no one and designing your course in such a way as to increase its usefulness to all students.

For a complete list of the guidelines, go to the Web Accessibility Initiative (WAI) of the World Wide Web Consortium (W3C).

- The World Wide Web Consortium (W3C)
  http://www.w3.org

- The Web Accessibility Initiative (WAI)
  http://www.w3.org/WAI

Check the accessibility of your course.

As you develop your course, gauge your progress in designing for accessibility by using one of the tools available to you. For example, use

"Bobby," a service provided without charge by the Center for Applied Special Technology (CAST), designed to help course-builders like you identify access problems for individuals with disabilities.

The Center for Applied Special Technology is an educational, not-for-profit organization that attempts to increase access opportunities for all people, including those with disabilities.

- Center for Applied Special Technology (CAST)
  http://www.cast.org
- Bobby
  http://www.cast.org/bobby

Section 3:
Teach Your Online Course

You've assessed your preparedness to teach online, made necessary arrangements for technical and administrative support, and created design and delivery standards for your course. You've taken your course from its outline to full development of web pages that include multiple types of activities, make extensive use of the threaded discussion areas, and require student collaboration. Great job! Now you're ready to teach this beast. Or are you? In this section, we introduce the final *Essential Elements* that will prepare you for the act (and art) of teaching in the virtual world.

Essential Element 14: Provide a comprehensive set of informational materials.

In the brick and mortar world, information about your course is passed on to students via catalog descriptions, guidance counselors, other teachers, or fellow students. Often, though, students sign up based on the title or a description alone, confident that they have a fairly accurate sense of what the course will entail. Online courses are different. Many students will never have experienced one before and have very little understanding of what they are getting into. It is essential that students receive accurate information about your course and what it entails before they enroll. They should have a clear understanding of what is expected, and whether your online course sounds right for them. Once students are in your course, be sure you include a set of documents that provides all the information about the course they will need.

Send advance information to students

Is online learning right for your students?

Have prospective students look at a demo course and/or take a questionnaire designed to help them determine if an online course is right for them. Several questionnaires are available that allow students to assess their learning preferences (asking such questions as, "How well do you work independently?" or "What technology background do you have?"). These questionnaires enable the would-be online student to evaluate whether or not an online course will meet their needs at this time. Take a similar quiz yourself at PBS Adult Learning Service:

http://www.pbs.org/als/college/dlandyou/quiz.htm

Make it known.

Make sure the students understand the course is online, and exactly what that means. Students need to understand that they might never meet you or other students face-to-face (unless you have built in some local, synchronous elements). In pre-course literature, emphasize that an online course is a "real" course that will require as much, or perhaps more, of a commitment (and self motivation) as an equivalent course they attend in person.

Provide students and guidance counselors/student advisors with the following information:

- The course description, prerequisites, hardware minimum requirements, software, browser, plug-ins, and download requirements. Describe what audio/video is included in the course, and the resulting required bandwidth/connection speed.

- A detailed list of the resources that schools and/or students will be required to provide or purchase, including those costs, as well as where and how to obtain the materials.

- A list of dates and times of any synchronous activities you require of them.

- Your add/drop/refund policies.

- An index with definitions of acronyms and technical terms that will be used in your course to help students understand what they read in the first few days.

Communicate your technology requirements.

Advertise the minimum technical skills students will need, and/or provide methods to learn them. Even if it's as basic as understanding how to use a web browser, let students know just what techniques they will be expected to know and perform technically. You don't want students who are overly frustrated by the technology from the beginning simply because they didn't know what was expected. They are likely to be those who drop out.

Communicate the time commitment.

Advertise the estimated time commitment students will need in order to take the course. Consider using a sliding scale, which reflects different Internet connection speeds. Let students know that if they are working on a slower modem (even if it's at or above the "minimal" level), it may take them longer to complete assignments. For example, tell students that, if they will be using a cable Internet connection to access the course, the assignments will require 8 to 10 hours per week; if they are on a modem, assignments could take 12 or more hours each week.

Communicate your participation requirements.

Tell students how many days per week they will be required to check into the course or post comments or work. Explain that participation equals posting and that "lurking" (logging on but not posting) will not be allowed. Courseware applications often allow instructors to see when and even where a student has logged into the course, but this information is essentially meaningless when it comes to student learning. The true learning comes from collaboration with other students, and that means posting to each other — not simply logging into the course site. If students are reading pages but not posting, they are not part of the class. Make your expectations explicit.

Gather information about your students.

As students register, gather their email addresses, snail mail addresses, and phone numbers. Verify all email addresses work before the course begins. See the next tip!

Send out welcoming email.

You can easily test your students' email addresses for accuracy by sending them the pre-course mailing(s). This important communication sets the stage for friendly, just-in-time information. A hearty welcome letter shows students you are preparing for them, that they are important to your course, and it reminds them of the start date and other important details.

Either in the initial welcome or a follow-up informational mailing, include the course's URL, the student's login name and password, how to obtain technical support, and how to contact you with course questions. (*Note:* Email formatting should be kept to a minimum, as many email programs won't interpret bold or italic text, for instance. Use asterisks, or lines made with the "hyphen" keystroke, for simple formatting instead.)

Agree to a Learning Support Agreement.

Another important document we recommend you send out is a Learning Support Agreement. This document details your expectations and requirements of your students (and what they can expect from you), including the minimum level of required participation and the estimated time commitment, as well as your grading policy, tuition refund and drop policy information. Ask your students to read and acknowledge their acceptance of your terms prior to the start of class to let you know that they are serious about being an online student in your course. Not receiving a response from a student on this mailing is a helpful indicator that they may not be ready to start the course, and allows you a head start to getting them on track. (See our sample on the following pages.)

Include course orientation, objectives, requirements, and criteria

Do you hand out introductory materials to students when your face-to-face course starts? Do you spend the first day of class going over your course policies and expectations? Perhaps you do this orally or perhaps you hand out an information packet that all students must read. In an online course, everything must be clearly presented in writing in a central location, and you'll need to provide at least the same information on the same topics you'd normally provide in a face-to-face class.

Post a course information packet.

As one of the very first lessons of your course, require students to read the "course packet" information. Keep it together and organized inside one centralized area of your course, so students can refer back to

Learning Support Agreement for Online Pedagogy Education

An online course offered by The Concord Consortium, September 19 — October 30, 2001

Please read this document carefully, as we detail both our expectations of you and what you can expect from us - the instructors and staff of the project. If you've never taken an online course before, you're in for a grand ride! To make this experience as positive and successful as possible, we'd like to set guidelines that we can all agree upon.

Once you've read the Learning Support Agreement, please send a short reply email, so we know you've read it and agree to its terms (don't worry, it's non-binding legally, but it lets both us and you know that you're serious about taking the course and will participate regularly in class). Feel free to print and keep a copy for yourself, storing it where you can find it for reference. Now may be the time to start a course folder that you'll continue to add to during the course.

Introductory emails

You will receive a series of email messages, welcoming you to the course and outlining the steps you need to take before starting class. You are responsible for making sure you'll have consistent access to at least one computer with an Internet connection and a recent version of the Internet Explorer browser installed before the course begins on Wednesday, September 19. Be sure to have Internet Explorer installed on all computers you plan to use.

Course URL and server maintenance

The URL for access to the course will remain constant throughout the term (we'll send that to you just before the course opens). Please note that the server that houses our courses has scheduled maintenance time every Tuesday evening from 5 to 6 p.m. Eastern Standard Time - the course may be unavailable during this time.

Communication

The primary method for communicating with the instructors will be making postings within the actual course. Occasionally, when either you or the instructors have an urgent issue that needs to be discussed or, during the opening weeks of class, using email will be appropriate. Our response time to your questions will be between 24 and 48 hours (or occasionally 72 hours, if over a weekend).

Class materials

As a participant, you'll receive two books (covered as part of your tuition):

* *Building Learning Communities in Cyberspace: Effective Strategies for the Online Classroom*

* *Facilitating Online Learning: Effective Strategies for Moderators*

Time commitment

Generally, it is assumed you'll spend approximately five to seven hours per week working on class assignments and participating in class discussions. Ideally, you'll be able to log in briefly every day and, at the absolute minimum, three times a week. Whatever your schedule, we expect you to show up regularly each week, and make substantial, thoughtful posts on at least three different days each week.

Participation

Participation in the course is required. We define participation as you posting discussion comments and assignments in the course (which we'll make clear once you start the course). If you just read course materials and discussions without posting yourself, you have not yet met your responsibilities. Participants learn in collaboration with one another, and your classmates can only *see* you through your comments in the Discussion Boards. Your classmates will need you to do your part to fulfill theirs. If, for any reason, you anticipate an upcoming absence during the course, we expect you to let us know as soon as possible, so we can plan for your absence and avoid assigning you to a team project or leadership role during that time. The success of the group depends on each of your personal commitments to making collaboration work!

Technical support

For Internet connectivity questions, you should check first with your local ISP provider. Course instructors will be available to assist you with registration, navigating the course, and other course-related issues.

Class announcements

We'll post weekly announcements for the entire class inside the course. Please watch for announcements as you first enter the course each time you log in. We may also email the group with general announcements.

Feedback

We will provide weekly feedback to all participants on their progress in the course, including feedback on participation, specific assignments, and group work. A passing grade in the course qualifies you to receive a certificate of completion.

Refunds

After registration, there will be no refunds for non-participation. You may, however, within one week of the course opening, substitute another person in your place, if you're unable to participate.

Post-course access

The course, including all class materials and discussions, will remain accessible to you and your classmates for one week following the end of class (through November 6). Your instructors will be unable to moderate any discussions that occur after the close of the course.

Please reply to this email (to Cynthia at cynthia@concord.org and Alese at alese@concord.org) with an accepting statement, so we know you have read - and agreed to the terms of - this LSA. Feel free to write with any questions.

Thank you.

it easily (most courseware allows you to use a separate area for these types of documents). Encourage students to print out these materials, too, just as they'd get them as hard copy if your course were an onsite course.

At a minimum, you should:

- Start the course with a **welcome letter** from you, including an introduction and a general overview of the course. Write in a friendly, positive, and helpful tone. Your students may be anxious, as online learning will be new to many of them. Help alleviate any fears from the beginning and model the tone you expect from them — friendly, encouraging, respectful.

- Provide a **syllabus** for the entire course in a week-by- week format, with learning objectives and due dates listed for major projects and important assessments.

- Post a **reading list** and a list of other required and recommended materials.

- Provide a thorough description of your **grading policy**, including grade categories (e.g., discussion participation, quizzes, tests, written work, lab work, team projects, individual projects; how categories/assignments are weighted; how to pass and how to earn an A; rules for late or missing work, details on the quality of work expected, how flexible you will be with due dates, and the consequences of late work).

- Advertise a complete **communication plan** for the course, including contact information for you and for technical assistance, and describe how students should ask both routine questions and deal with emergencies within your course. Include your phone number and office hours for students to contact you in the case of an emergency (e.g., messages such as the computer ate their homework, their Internet service provider is unavailable, personal illness, or an urgent family matter).

- Provide a statement of **student expectations** that includes topics like the minimum log in pattern, a list of things to do at each log in, and a description of appropriate behavior.

Think about your tone of voice.

If you normally communicate your expectations and policies orally, it may be a bit of a challenge to "translate" what you say into writing. You will want to set a positive tone right from the beginning, to encourage engaged, active learning and to let students know that you are accessible to them. For example, you might use a bit of humor in your face-to-face class to get across important points; try to do the same in your writing. No one likes reading dry lists of rules and regulations. Aim to make your introductory documents engaging and fun, while at the same time conveying their importance. You will have no facial expressions to go by, so you will have to convey yourself and the tone of the course entirely through your words. Graphics and emoticons work wonders to lighten text.

Essential Element 15: Facilitate discussions in a way that keeps students on-task, promotes full participation, and encourages peer collaboration.

As an instructor, you will have many roles, the most important of which, perhaps, is the facilitator of course discussions, as that is where the learning happens. Read our tips below for both the "behind the scenes" and the more visible work you will do to create effective discussions in your course.

Promote participation

Include a minimum posting requirement.

Although we suggest end-of-the-week due dates for individual assignments, we also suggest including a general posting requirement in your course. This means that you let students know that you expect them to come to class and make their presence felt via "posting" on a minimum number of days each and every week. We usually set three separate days per week as our minimum posting requirement. Without this, your class discussions can falter, with students all waiting until the end of the week to "say" something. In addition to the weekly posting requirements, state posting requirements for each individual lesson (e.g., at least one reply to the main starter thread, plus at least one comment in response to a peer).

Postings can consist of everything from required check-ins (where students simply let you know they are working), to thoughtful contributions to a discussion on a particular topic (a required reading, for example). Within this guideline, students should be encouraged to post to each other as part of the requirement, so that they are reading and responding to what their peers are saying, and not just telling the teacher the answers they may think are required.

Forbid lurking/auditing of the course.

Structure the course so that regular, ongoing written participation is required. Provide plenty of opportunity in your lessons for this type of active participation. Students will benefit most from a course with full participation in a discussion. If only a half, or perhaps a third, of the students are regular contributors to a discussion thread, the viewpoint of all those lurkers is necessarily left out. You will want everyone to chime in with their opinions of the reading and the activities. Students learn by sharing their thoughts with each other, bouncing ideas off each other, and engaging in a true dialogue. When students share in this way, they construct knowledge together, and this is the type of learning that sticks. They will be able to apply this knowledge in new situations, as they have experienced the knowledge personally, and not just as a memorization feat.

Encourage participation throughout the week.

Timing is different than in a face-to-face course, so plan and allow for it. Discussions take longer because students get online at their own pace, so it is conceivable that a single class discussion between students all in the same room could become a week-long discussion in an online course. Encourage students to post early in the week and then return to the discussion area often, to look for replies to their initial posts and to engage further in the dialogue with others.

Remind students of the Learning Support Agreement, if participation is lagging.

Students signed — or should have signed — a Learning Support Agreement, in which they agreed to participate a minimum number of days each week. If students neglect to fulfill their end of the bargain, feel free to gently remind them of the LSA (see a sample Learning Support Agreement in *Essential Element 14*).

Structure your communications

Communicate in the course.

Emphasize that all communication should take place inside the course and not through email (except for emergencies). This allows you to maintain a complete record of all communications related to the course, keeps you in the loop of all student-to-student conversations, provides a single place to look for course-related communications, and keeps everyone's email in-boxes less chaotic.

Emergency communications.

Provide and advertise alternative means of communication for emergencies, for situations when students' or your course provider's server is unavailable. Advertise a comprehensive communication plan, detailing the routine methods of communication and those to use in emergencies.

Make private space.

Create a discussion area that provides a private thread for each student. Restrict access to each of these threads to just you and an individual student, allowing for private and individual communication between the two of you. Here you will discuss grades and evaluations, absences, personal problems, and other matters. Consider creating an assignment for your students to post to their private space — to make sure they know where it is and how to use it.

Create ongoing threads.

Provide and advertise discussion threads for technical questions, another for questions to clarify the assignments or content, and a third for informal and personal student conversations unrelated to the course (the coffee klatch — see *Essential Element 8*). The first two allow students to alert you to their questions and the third allows an online community to grow. Check into the "questions" threads daily and aim for immediate turnarounds so that students' questions don't prevent them from completing assignments on time, build frustrations, or lose momentum.

Create weekly check-in threads.

Students need a place to vent or, conversely, to cheer. Create a special thread — weekly or bi-weekly — for this purpose. We entitle ours "Let's Talk" to emphasize the open sharing and debriefing nature of this thread. Encourage students to share what they're learning about themselves as online learners, what they like about the activities, and what they are finding to be challenging (see also *Essential Element 17*).

Create topical threads.

Each week (or module), you will have one or more discussions devoted to a specific topic, for example, a reading, a web search, or a problem set. Seed the discussion with a "starter thread," in which you ask expansive questions and open the dialogue to students. Direct students to read your post first and respond there, rather than to create new threads. You will have a more organized discussion board this way, where learning can happen more effectively.

Everything has a purpose.

Create a separate thread (discussion posting) for each purpose, and advertise those purposes clearly. If there are two (or more) major discussion topics for the week, they should be separated. For instance, a discussion on a virtual frog dissection should take place in a different location from the question and answer session regarding Chapter 2 of the biology book students were assigned to read. Let students know that each of their postings will have a target thread in which to appear (e.g., "Virtual Frog Dissection Discussion" or "Chapter 2 Reading"); that each question will have an appropriate destination (e.g., "Questions on Technical Issues"); and that it is important for students to use them correctly.

Different roles for different threads.

Your role will be different and will require different responses, depending on the purpose of the discussion thread. If a thread's purpose is to answer students' questions, a quick response is essential. Some student postings, on the other hand, will require no response at all from you. The types of discussions where a teacher responds with a simple "OK" (or even a slight nod of the head, in an onsite class) as a checkmark or an indication to move along are not helpful in an online course — and can serve to kill a discussion. Discussions online should never be done as a filler. Your responses need to be qualitative.

If it's newsworthy, let your students know.

In addition to the communication in your course's threaded discussions, make it a habit to provide frequent announcements to your students in a prominent course area. Whether you decide to use weekly or even daily announcements, keep your students apprized of breaking news, changes to assignments or due dates, solutions to common problems, updates on situations, alerts to particular students — whatever information needs to be communicated. Don't assume the lessons and student communications will be sufficient. News happens.

Send special purpose emails.

When you need to contact an individual or small group of students, consider an email rather than a full-class announcement. For instance, during group work, contact team leaders by email with a special note describing their role, the start dates, how to get additional support, and so forth. (*Hint:* Save your messages, as they will become templates for the next round of your course.)

Encourage collaboration

Design collaboration through discussion.

Use the discussion feature of the course extensively, routinely requiring students to interact with each other on the content topics you introduce in the course. Discussion facilitates interaction among the students, instead of single responses back to the teacher. Plan lessons for this to happen, so you can stay out of the middle and allow students to learn from each other.

Ask for opinions.

Routinely encourage students to share their multiple viewpoints and their opinions as part of their collaborative work. You have a course full of different voices; let them be heard, to optimize the learning potential.

Encourage peer feedback.

It takes much more time to type out responses to each student's submissions than it does to engage in the same discussion in a class where students communicate verbally. Because of that, build in ways for students to provide feedback to each other, instead of your trying to answer all questions and comment on all submissions personally.

Facilitate discussions

Moderate well for effective learning.

Use different voices in your responses to students — conceptual facilitator, personal muse, or role-player. Use different tones as well, from nurturing to neutral, whimsical to analytical, to fit the situation. The idea is to encourage, to draw out, to correct behavior, to calm, to dig deeper. (And be sure to read *Facilitating Online Learning: Effective Strategies for Moderators* [Collison et al. 2000], for the quintessential moderating strategies.)

Check your posts repeatedly for tone by re-reading each comment before you post it to the discussion board.

Communicate appropriately.

Use the appropriate method of communication to meet the particular need at hand. For instance, although your course is online and you want to encourage most communication to take place within the course discussion board, there are occasions when phone calls may be the most effective and efficient method to cut to the chase. Alternative means of communication are especially important when students drop from sight or are having technical problems that are not getting resolved through a sincere effort in the appropriate technical question thread.

Reflect student ideas.

One of the most useful functions of a moderator is that of a reflector of ideas. The meaning of "reflector" is taken directly from the physical analog — that is, mirroring. The moderator should consider making posts that simply highlight particularly interesting or perhaps fruitful lines of dialogue. Offer them up without praise or added value, but muse about them with the purpose of exploring potential meanings. Any questions you pose should be partially answered in the musing. The purpose of such a post is to model the airing of internal dialogue that can form the heart of a fruitful asynchronous discussion.

Let students direct the learning.

Ask students to submit their lists of critical questions on the subject at hand. Compile the best of these questions and, in the next activity, ask students to answer them. This allows students to help direct the learning. Also consider using surveys to assess student understanding or to poll students for their ideas (e.g., reordering discussion threads, changing the focus or due date of an assignment, among others).

Respond quickly to questions.

Your role as the "guide on the side" will call for your measured response. Rather than jumping into each discussion, you will select your interventions carefully, noting where they might be most useful to move the discussion further along. With technical or assignment questions, however, you should aim to make your feedback as quickly as possible. Respond within 24 hours and, if an answer is not available, try to at least acknowledge the question, with a promise to research the problem within a set period of time.

Avoid letter writing.

Language makes a difference in fostering collaboration. In your responses to posts, avoid a tone than mimics that of a personal letter, which might typically begin, "Thanks, Toni, for making that point." Such a format may read to other students like a private discussion, and unintentionally serve to inhibit them from taking part in the dialogue. Aim, instead, to include your full class audience with a general statement, like "Toni points out... ." Students will be more inclined to join the conversation if they feel welcomed and included.

Essential Element 16: Engage your students without over-engaging.

How you engage with your students is one of the most important aspects of online teaching. Whether or not you designed the course, you're the one to teach your students. That engagement — both in terms of the quality and quantity of the interaction — is central to the learning process.

Learn to remove yourself from the middle of the discussions.

You've heard the expression "guide on the side" and you know what it means; now is the time and place to put this teaching strategy into action (or non-action, as the case may be). Students will learn more by your strategically timed and placed moderator interventions than by short comments to each post. They will stay tuned and look for your thought-provoking comments, while engaging in a focused dialogue with each other. Keep in mind that guiding on the side does not mean you are on the sidelines, not allowed to interact with the players. In fact, you are a key player!

Don't feel you have to comment on every posting that every student makes.

Not only do you not *have* to do this, you simply *shouldn't*. This sets up student expectations for the frequency and types of postings you will make. Students will be less likely to respond to each other (and certainly not with anything of depth), and your course will be relegated to one in which students hand in their work. Build this understanding/ expectation into your course early: You won't respond to every posting;

other classmates are to respond, instead. Reflect on student work without providing the "answer" or "teacher knows all" approach.

Avoid getting into continuous conversations with each student.

Don't allow yourself to get involved with multiple back-and-forths with students. Multiple, individual comments to you in the discussion threads are the equivalent of a demanding in-box full of email messages to you from your students. Run screaming! This situation sets up the rest of your students to just read and watch, and resembles a correspondence course, not one where student collaboration is at the center of the learning. Don't spend your time unnecessarily. Keep the conversations primarily between students.

Assure students you are reading all their posts, even if you don't comment.

Assure students that you will read and note every contribution they make even if you don't comment to each one individually. Explain to students that they may not get immediate responses or any peer responses at all to some comments in a discussion, but this is normal in an asynchronous environment and they shouldn't take it personally. If students contribute actively and regularly, they will receive meaningful comments on at least some of their postings. When students follow up on comments to their posts, they take the discussion deeper.

Wait it out.

Responses to your own queries or posts will not be immediate; communications may take hours or days. That's part of the asynchronous world. That's the down side. The flip side, of course, is that responses are more likely to be thoughtful, deeply reflective comments rather than the spur of the moment comments that might occur in a face-to-face course. Be patient with your students and with the nature of asynchronous threaded discussions — you are sure to be pleased with the outcome.

Make yourself and your students heard.

Give tips for ways students can make sure their comments get responses, for example, by using short, descriptive comment titles in online communications, and including the target student's name in the title if the post is to one person, or a specific group. Also explain how to use a discussion thread most effectively, which includes encouraging posting as early in the week as possible, and then checking in and responding to others throughout the week; asking thoughtful questions; using interesting, anecdotal examples in your writing; thinking about how your grammar and spelling comes across to others; being respectful and interested in what others have to say; and talking about examples and topics that you personally find interesting and that come from real life.

There's a time and place for everything.

Differentiate between the types of communication possible, or needed. There are places and times for private conversations with each student; there are also places and times that the instructor is guide on the side, mostly quiet, letting students communicate with each other about the content of the course, which helps them learn from, and with, each other.

Think about the way you present yourself to students face-to-face.

Are you serious and strict, or good-natured and funny? If you like to use humor in your face-to-face class, by all means use humor online. But do think about how your humor may come across and consider new ways to express your funny side. Some jokes or gags may not work well without accompanying facial cues or body language. Sometimes things meant as a joke fall flat in plain black and white text. Try using visual aids in the form of accompanying graphics, lightening things up with colors, pictures, and emoticons. As always, you'll want to make sure it's appropriate. If using humor, be respectful of other cultures. Also, watch for signs of student reaction. While you can't see students smile or laugh online, you can read their words (or note their absence).

Essential Element 17: Assess student work and provide student feedback.

Providing feedback to online participants is critical for a number of reasons: letting students know how they are doing; commenting on individual student contributions and course work (which does not happen in the discussion board); and keeping students engaged. You may decide to use quizzes and exams, or base student grades solely on participation in the discussion threads.

State your expectations.

Clearly state what is expected for a passing grade on every assignment and activity in the course. Be sure you state the manner in which your students will be assessed on all assignments, including rubrics and point values. Specify expectations in terms of quality and quantity. If you will be relying on student participation as the sole means for evaluation, include a rubric for participation, clearly detailing acceptable types of posts. Provide sample posts, where appropriate.

Provide frequent, predictable feedback to students.

Students want to know how they are doing, especially when they don't have the benefit of a quick approving glance from you or an informal verbal evaluation after class. Provide this information in the form of weekly or bi-weekly evaluations to your students. Use the following checklist to guide the evaluation process:

- **Create an evaluation table** — listing the different assignments as column headers at the top of a table and all the participant names in the rows beneath — or use a hard copy grade book to keep track of each student's work.

- **Create an evaluation template.** Develop a generic template each week that can be copied and pasted for everyone, yet that is open-ended and flexible enough to allow you to fill in personal details. Make them positive, assuming the best; then personalize as appropriate.

- **Check participant work.** Using your table or grade book, check off each activity that a student has completed. (*Hint:* If your courseware offers a "sort by" field in its threaded discussion, use it to search for each student's posts.)

- **Post evaluations.** Post evaluations to each student in their private discussion space, so that only they and you have access to this information.

Make student evaluations accessible.

Make available clear and up-to-date records of each student's progress within the course, and update them at least bi-weekly (or more frequently if the course is shorter than semester length). Explain where, how, and when students can check their grades, as well as where students can ask questions on their evaluations.

Quote your students.

Each week, choose a great quote from each student and cite that in your assessment of their work. This lets them know that although you may not respond to each comment they make, you are reading all comments and making note of important contributions they have made. Your software may allow a sorting "by student" or "by author," so you can easily review contributions by each student, one at a time. Or take notes of important contributions during the week, to easily paste into a student's evaluation at the end of the week.

Consider using your courseware's assessment features.

Most courseware on the market includes a variety of assessment tools. Although you will likely find the usual true/false, fill in the blank, and short answer types of questions, don't rely on these too heavily. While fine for evaluating a variety of different types of information, they are not any better in an online course than they are face-to-face. Also, they are often time consuming and frustrating for your students, so keep these types of tests short and far between. Because students are on the web as they're taking your quiz/test, consider them "open book," unless you're able to proctor them. Use short answer or essay questions to eliminate worries about cheating; you will know students' online "voices" and be able to gauge their learning.

Use self-assessments.

Use self-assessments to replace quizzes, especially if your goal is for students to gauge for themselves their learning on a set of facts. Self-assessments have the added benefit of saving you the time of grading, since most courseware allows them to be scored automatically. Students are provided with the information to reflect on their work and achievements (or areas for improvement), or with the technical or other factual answers that you are testing. Encourage students to take the self-assessment before searching the web or your course site for answers. Suggest that students review the answers and follow up with appropriate resources that help them learn the material they didn't know.

Encourage public self-assessments.

Consider using public self-assessments as another option for students to think about their learning, apart from a formal grade from you, the instructor. Encourage students to share what they are learning

---

Grading Elements

- You have an introductory document that explains your grading guidelines for students and where in your course students will find their grades.

- You include learning objectives for each activity in your course.

- You state what is expected of students for a passing grade on every assignment and activity in your course.

- You provide assessments throughout the course that are appropriate to the subject matter.

- You record, post, and make available to students, in some type of gradebook or other private area, all of their grades, including completed and not completed assignments, and general grades on areas like participation or teamwork.

- You create a private discussion area for each student as a place where they can ask you questions about their grades or any other questions of a private nature.

- You create exams or quizzes, if the courseware allows, and post the returned grades.

- You provide opportunities for student self-assessment by encouraging students to reflect on their own learning in a public or private space, or by more structured self-assessments.

---

about themselves as online learners. This might take the form of an optional weekly thread devoted to this purpose. (See *Essential Element 15* for more on weekly check-in threads.)

Think differently about assessments.

Use assessments throughout the course that are appropriate to the subject matter, based on stated learning objectives, and clearly indicate student mastery. Consider portfolio assessment, for instance, where students compile their best products. Alternatively, some situations might benefit from performance assessment. For example, in a performing arts course, ask students to identify a local panel for whom they perform. Provide a set of grading rubrics for the panel and ask that they rate and report student performance back to you.

Summary

You picked up this book because you wanted to know more about designing and teaching an online course — and you wanted just the *Essential Elements* plus a set of tangible tips you could easily implement. You probably had a number of questions about online teaching, and perhaps were feeling confused and anxious about the prospect of developing a course and teaching in the virtual environment.

To answer some of these questions and allay your concerns, we have presented you with seventeen *Essential Elements* as well as countless tips for implementing those elements into your online course. We are confident this is the best advice you'll find on preparing, designing, and teaching an online course, and hope we have been able to communicate this information to you in a way that will allow you to get busy immediately and produce a successful course.

Our hope is that you've taken advantage of the Essential Checklist in Appendix C to record your good ideas and chart your progress in key areas, noting any questions and to-do items. As you have learned, there are many issues to consider when planning and designing an online course, and there is much to set in order before you can begin.

On the other hand, as the time for delivery of your course approaches, don't worry if you haven't checked every item off your list. If you focus first on the most important requirements for your course, you can work through the remaining tips later, as time allows. There may well be some you will not implement at all during the first running of your course, instead adding them over time.

If you're an experienced face-to-face teacher or trainer, think back to your first class. Remember how excited you were? How frightened? Think about how little you knew then compared to what you know now. As with that first face-to-face class, there is much here for you to learn and experience over time. Realize that the nervousness and awkwardness you may be feeling is only the first stage in learning about something new. Now comes the rewarding part of experiencing online teaching firsthand. With this book as a guide, you are in a position to go forward and begin your new adventure, feeling confident.

We wish you every virtual (and real!) success.

Appendix A:
Accessibility Websites

The following websites devote their attention to web accessibility issues.

Americans with Disabilities Act Home Page
http://www.usdoj.gov/crt/ada/adahom1.htm

This website from the U.S. Department of Justice includes information on the Americans with Disabilities Act, a guide to disability rights laws, technical assistance materials, and links to affiliated sites.

Equal Access to Software and Information (EASI)
http://www.easi.cc

EASI provides information and resources in the area of access-to-information technologies by individuals with disabilities. They also offer online training on adaptive technology and consulting services for schools and companies.

IBM Accessibility Center
http://www-3.ibm.com/able/accessweb.html

Use their checklist to make your website accessible. Their list includes checkpoints from the Word Wide Web Consortium (W3C), Web Accessibility Initiative found at www.w3.org/WAI. The matrix of topics includes links to the WAI rationales, as well as techniques for implementing the checkpoints.

OUACHITA TECHNICAL COLLEGE

National Center for Accessible Media
http://www.ncam.org

The CPB/WGBH National Center for Accessible Media (NCAM) is a research and development facility dedicated to the issues of media and information technology for people with disabilities.

Office of Special Education Programs (OSEP)
http://www.ed.gov/offices/OSERS/OSEP/Resources/link.html

This technical assistance and dissemination network site provides links to curriculum, publications, products, and programs for youth with disabilities.

Section 508 Home Page
http://www.usdoj.gov/crt/508/508home.html

This U.S. Department of Justice website defines Section 508, which requires that Federal agencies' electronic and information technology is accessible to people with disabilities, including employees and members of the public.

WebAIM
http://www.webaim.org

Web Accessibility In Mind (WebAIM) aims to improve accessibility to online learning opportunities for all people, particularly for individuals with disabilities.

Appendix B:
List of Resources

Carroll, T.G. 2000. If we didn't have the schools we have today, would we create the schools we have today? *Contemporary Issues in Technology and Teacher Education, 1*(1), 117—140. Available: http://www.citejournal.org/vol1/iss1/currentissues/general/article1.htm

Collison, George, Bonnie Elbaum, Sarah Haavind, and Robert Tinker. 2000. *Facilitating online learning: Effective strategies for moderators*. Madison, WI: Atwood Publishing.

The Concord Consortium. 2000. *Inquiryworks! Real teachers, real stories*. Rowley, MA: The Network.

Donovan, M. Suzanne, John D. Bransford, and James W. Pellegrino (eds.). 1999. *How people learn: Bridging research and practice*. Washington, DC: National Academy Press.

Hanna, Donald E., Michelle Glowacki-Dudka, and Simone Conceicao- Runlee. 2000. *147 Practical tips for teaching online groups: Essentials of web-based education*. Madison, WI: Atwood Publishing.

The Institute for Higher Education Policy. 2000. *Quality on the line: Benchmarks for success in internet-based distance education*. Washington, DC: The Institute for Higher Education Policy.

Ko, Susan, and Steve Rossen. 2001. *Teaching online: A practical guide*. Boston: Houghton Mifflin.

Palloff, Rena M., and Keith Pratt. 1999. *Building learning communities in cyberspace: Effective strategies for the classroom*. San Francisco: Jossey-Bass.

Palloff, Rena M., and Keith Pratt. 2001. *Lessons from the cyberspace classroom: The realities of online teaching*. San Francisco: Jossey-Bass.

White, Ken W., and Bob H. Weight. 2000. *The online teaching guide: A handbook of attitudes, strategies, and techniques for the virtual classroom*. Needham Heights, MA: Allyn & Bacon.

Appendix C:
Essential Checklist

ESSENTIAL CHECKLIST		
Section 1. Prepare for Your Online Course		
Essential Element 1: **Prepare to teach online.**		
	Your Notes	
Take an online course.		☐
Be excited!		☐
Panic if you must.		☐
Believe in the outcome.		☐
Do your homework.		☐
Know your stuff.		☐
Set aside the time.		☐
Learn to express yourself in text.		☐
You are more than a teacher.		☐

Essential Element 2: Build a course outline.		
	Your Notes	
List your course objectives.		☐
Develop an outline.		☐
Add bullets to your outline.		☐
Create a timeline for developing your course.		☐
Keep your start date in mind.		☐
Plan time to convert a face-to-face course.		☐
Plan (more) time to create a new course.		☐

Essential Element 3: Create a course schedule with clear deadlines.		
	Your Notes	
Choose your basic time unit.		☐
Decide when your weeks begin and end.		☐
Determine the length of your course.		☐
Plan the workload.		☐
Don't count technical time.		☐
Think about the pace.		☐
What's the critical mass?		☐
Will you have synchronous meetings? Or not?		☐

Essential Element 4: **Plan for ongoing quality assurance.**		
	Your Notes	
Create standards.		☐
Encourage student feedback.		☐
Request anonymous evaluations.		☐
Welcome a mentor or peer.		☐
Keep a journal of your online teaching experience.		☐
Host an open forum.		☐
Provide an end-of-course evaluation.		☐
Essential Element 5: **Ensure support from your administration.**		
	Your Notes	
It takes a team to offer online courses.		☐
Develop policies and procedures.		☐
Provide organizational services.		☐
Provide adequate staffing support for course-builders, teachers, and students.		☐
Develop and enforce course standards and quality control.		☐
Provide ongoing professional development.		☐
Essential Element 6: **Provide technical support.**		
	Your Notes	
Start with yourself.		☐

Essential Element 6: Provide technical support (con't).		
Practice patience in the face of (technological) adversity.		☐
Know your audience.		☐
Walk in a student's shoes.		☐
Give good directions — Part I.		☐
Give good directions — Part II.		☐
Give good directions — Part III.		☐
Make time for learning the technology.		☐
Don't use technology just because you can.		☐
Don't use the courseware's capabilities just because they exist.		☐
Use the courseware features to best suit your needs.		☐
Provide technical support for your students.		☐
Advertise how to get help.		☐
Make it visible.		☐
Consider a technical FAQ document.		☐

Section 2. Design your online course

Essential Element 7: Format your course so that students can focus on the content.		
	Your Notes	
Create document templates.		☐
Use clip art where appropriate.		☐

Essential Element 7: **Format your course so that students can focus on the content (con't).**		
Let your personality shine.		☐
Use animations sparingly.		☐
Adopt a consistent, sensible layout for all your documents.		☐
Keep it generic? Or personalize?		☐
Converting is not just transferring materials.		☐
Essential Element 8: **Design a learning community that is collaborative, engaging, and inclusive.**		
	Your Notes	
First, build trust.		☐
State the community expectations.		☐
Put communication first.		☐
Start off on the right foot.		☐
Get acquainted.		☐
Continue to get personal.		☐
Coffee klatch, anyone?		☐
You are a part of the community, too.		☐
Tone it down.		☐
Introduce small group work when it's time.		☐
Be sensitive to your students.		☐

Essential Element 9:
Find and use appropriate course materials and resources.

	Your Notes	
Just because a course is online, it doesn't mean all your materials have to be.		☐
Find new online resources.		☐
Find it electronically and save a tree.		☐
Get permission.		☐
Consider lending materials.		☐
Reach out to different learners.		☐
Gather first.		☐
Create a set of additional resource links.		☐

Essential Element 10:
Develop rich, relevant activities to support your learning objectives.

	Your Notes	
Use a learning cycle.		☐
Create weekly overviews.		☐
Can they swallow it whole?		☐
A single activity only, please.		☐
Recast each activity for the online context.		☐
Detail, detail, detail.		☐
Test your instructions.		☐
What's the grade?		☐

Essential Element 10: Develop rich, relevant activities to support your learning objectives (con't).		
Make it personal		☐
Variety is the spice of life.		☐
Repeat yourself.		☐
Plan activities that require student collaboration.		☐
Advertise the due date.		☐
Essential Element 11: Include a balanced mixture of individual and group learning activities.		
	Your Notes	
Individual activities		
Private versus public.		☐
Handing in work.		☐
A little bit every week.		☐
Get off the computer.		☐
Provide prompt feedback.		☐
Group activities		
Achieve balance.		☐
Make it collaborative		☐
Divide activities into separate parts.		☐
Create supporting materials in advance.		☐
Group similar students together? Or not?		☐

Essential Element 11: Include a balanced mixture of individual and group learning activities (con't).		
How big is just right?		☐
Include clear instructions.		☐
Group work takes time. Allow for it.		☐
When to use different groups.		☐
Flavor it international.		☐
Allow time to digest.		☐
Essential Element 12: Recognize that pacing in an online course is different.		
	Your Notes	
Begin slowly.		☐
Let students get their feet wet first.		☐
Plan multiple activities.		☐
Schedule for asynchronicity.		☐
Divide and conquer.		☐
Provide check-in points.		☐
Redefine due dates.		☐
Essential Element 13: Provide equal accessibility to all students.		
	Your Notes	
Follow the Web Content Accessibility Guidelines.		☐
Check the accessibility of your course.		☐

Section 3. Teach your online course		
Essential Element 14: **Provide a comprehensive set of informational materials.**		
	Your Notes	
Send advance information to students.		
Is online learning right for your students?		☐
Make it known.		☐
Communicate your technology requirements.		☐
Communicate the timecommitment.		☐
Communicate your participation requirements.		☐
Gather information about your students.		☐
Send out welcoming email.		☐
Agree to a Learning Support Agreement.		☐
Essential Element 14: **Provide a comprehensive set of informational materials (con't).**		
Include course orientation, objectives, requirements, and criteria.		
Post a course information packet.		☐
Think about your tone of voice.		☐
Essential Element 15: **Facilitate discussions in a way that keeps students on-task, promotes full participation, and encourages peer collaboration.**		
	Your Notes	
Promote participation		
Include a minimum posting requirement.		☐

Essential Element 15: Facilitate discussions in a way that keeps students on-task, promotes full participation, and encourages peer collaboration (con't).		
Forbid lurking/auditing the course.		☐
Encourage participation throughout the week.		☐
Remind students of the Learning Support Agreement, if participation is lagging.		☐
Structure your communications		
Communicate in the course.		☐
Emergency communications.		☐
Make private space.		☐
Create ongoing threads.		☐
Create weekly check-in threads.		☐
Create topical threads.		☐
Everything has a purpose.		☐
Different roles for different threads.		☐
If it's newsworthy, let your students know.		☐
Send special purpose emails.		☐
Encourage collaboration		
Design collaboration through discussion.		☐
Ask for opinions.		☐
Encourage peer feedback.		☐
Facilitate discussions		

Essential Element 15:
Facilitate discussions in a way that keeps students on-task, promotes full participation, and encourages peer collaboration (con't).

Moderate well for effective learning.		☐
Communicate appropriately.		☐
Reflect student ideas.		☐
Let students direct the learning.		☐
Respond quickly to questions.		☐
Avoid letter writing.		☐

Essential Element 16:
Engage with your students without over-engaging.

	Your Notes	
Learn to remove yourself from the middle of the discussions.		☐
Don't feel you have to comment on every posting that every student makes.		☐
Avoid getting into continuous conversations with each student.		☐
Assure students you are reading all their posts, even if you don't comment.		☐
Wait it out.		☐
Make yourself and your students heard.		☐
There's a time and place for everything.		☐
Think about the way you present yourself to students face-to-face.		☐

Essential Element 17: Assess student work and provide feedback.		
	Your Notes	
State your expectations.		☐
Provide frequent, predictable feedback to students.		☐
Make student evaluations accessible.		☐
Quote your students.		☐
Consider using your courseware's assessment features.		☐
Use self-assessments.		☐
Encourage public self-assessments.		☐
Think differently about assessments.		☐

About the Authors

Bonnie Elbaum designs and teaches professional development NetCourses for the Virtual High School, Inc. and The Concord Consortium. She also researches and writes about online education; she has co-authored articles on the subject, as well as a book, *Facilitating Online Learning: Effective Strategies for Moderators*.

Cynthia McIntyre has designed and facilitated professional development courses for INTEC, the Virtual High School and The Concord Consortium. She has written articles on online education and edited a book, *Inquiry Works! Real Teachers, Real Stories*, which highlights secondary teachers bringing inquiry into their classrooms.

Alese Smith has designed and facilitated professional development programs for the Virtual High School and for The Concord Consortium. She has presented at national conferences and conducted hands-on tutorials on effective online course design and delivery, as well as consulted with organizations on the skills and philosophies for successfully transforming face-to-face courses to the online venue.

The Concord Consortium (http://www.concord.org). The Concord Consortium — founded in 1994 in Concord, Massachusetts, by Dr. Robert Tinker — is a nonprofit educational technology lab dedicated to improving teaching practices through the appropriate integrated use of technology in the classroom. Through our many National Science Foundation, U.S. Department of Education, and privately funded projects, we have taught thousands of secondary students, as well as secondary and university educators and other professionals over the Internet. We have also helped hundreds of teachers transform their face-to-face (F2F) courses for the web and deliver them to their students.

We have been designing and offering courses since 1994, when we created the International Netcourse Teacher Enhancement Coalition (INTEC). INTEC offered a year-long professional development course for secondary teachers of mathematics and science, aimed at helping them bring more inquiry-oriented activities into their classrooms. In 1996, we offered our first Teachers Learning Conference, a 26-week online course, which trains secondary teachers in online teaching practices and prepares them to design and deliver their own online course in the Virtual High School. Participating schools contribute one course in exchange for twenty student seats in any course in the catalog as part of a cooperative model. VHS now offers courses to over five thousand students across the United States and around the globe.

Pioneers in online course development, the e-Learning Group at The Concord Consortium continues to create, develop, and implement innovative approaches to teaching and learning online.